History of the American Society of Missiology, 1973–2013

History of the American Society of Missiology, 1973–2013

Wilbert R. Shenk

Published by
Institute of Mennonite Studies

Library of Congress Cataloging-in-Publication Data

Shenk, Wilbert R.
  History of the American Society of Missiology, 1973–2013 / Wilbert R. Shenk.
    pages cm
  Includes bibliographical references.
  ISBN 0-936273-52-6
  1. American Society of Missiology—History. 2. Missions—Societies, etc. I.
Title.
  BV2010.S54 2014
  266.006'073—dc23
                          2014002580

History of the American Society of Missiology, 1973–2013

Copyright © 2014 by Institute of Mennonite Studies, Anabaptist Mennonite Biblical Seminary, 3003 Benham Avenue, Elkhart, IN 46517. All rights reserved.

International Standard Book Number: 0-936273-52-6

Printed by Duley Press, Mishawaka, Indiana

To order or request information, please call 1-574-296-6239 or email ims@ambs.edu.

Cost of this volume has been subsidized through the generosity of an anonymous donor.

With gratitude to American Society of Missiology founders
Ralph D. Winter (1924–2009)
and
Gerald H. Anderson
for their vision, fortitude, and wise leadership

Contents

Preface

In anticipation of the fortieth anniversary of the founding of the American Society of Missiology in 2013, in 2010 ASM president Robert Gallagher asked me to prepare a forty-year history of the society.

The experience over the past four decades has demonstrated clearly that if an organization is to serve its members, it must be responsive to its changing environment. The initiatives taken in the third and fourth decades to realign ASM structures and patterns to better serve its members are instructive. Rereading the official minutes and reports of the ASM board of directors, the members annual meetings, and the board of publications, one is reminded that a scholarly society depends on the volunteered labors of many people—editors, board members, planning committees, officers, and others. An effort has been made in the present account to draw attention to at least some of those who have served so faithfully and effectively.

As ASM embarks on its fifth decade, it does so with renewed energy and hope. The mission of God calls us to face and move toward the future, not the past. Yet that continuing pilgrimage should always be pursued with keen awareness of the generations of witnesses who have preceded us.

This fortieth anniversary account of the American Society of Missiology has built on the two previous editions. But an effort has been made to revise, update, and extend this history, highlighting both failures and achievements.

Wilbert R. Shenk
June 2013

1

The roots and emergence of mission studies

The founding of the American Society of Missiology in 1973 was a pivotal step in gaining academic recognition for the field of mission studies in North America. Before the twentieth century, study of the Christian mission was regarded as unworthy of academic attention. Missions were the preoccupation of fevered fanatics and foolhardy enthusiasts.

Nonetheless, early in the nineteenth century thoughtful missionaries and missions administrators recognized the need for guidance in carrying out the missionary mandate that might be gained through a disciplined and scientific study of the basis, methods, and goals of the Christian mission (Myklebust 1955, 1957). But proponents of mission studies were of a divided mind. On the one hand, the pioneers of the movement were imbued with a sense of both the urgency and the magnitude of the task. It called for action rather than reflection, for practical application instead of theoretical constructs. Mission training schools were expected to prepare candidates for action, not reflection. On the other hand, those convinced that a rigorous scholarly understanding of missions was needed were frustrated by the marginal place assigned mission studies in the theological curriculum—be that of seminary or university. This marginalization was symptomatic of the persistently tenuous position of missions in the life of the church generally.

When the Presbyterian General Assembly approved the establishment of Princeton Theological Seminary in 1811, the proposal included provision for "a nursery for missionaries to the heathen" (Myklebust 1955, 146; see Beaver 1976). The seminary opened in 1812—but without missionary training. In 1830 the general assembly adopted a resolution "That there be appointed an additional Professor . . . to bear the name and title of the 'Professor of Pastoral Theology and Missionary instruction.'" In 1836 Charles Breckenridge was selected to fill this posi-tion, but in 1839 he took a position with the Board of Foreign Missions of the Presbyterian Church in the USA and no replacement for him at the seminary was appointed.

Early mission publications

From the early years of the modern mission movement, magazines and journals devoted to missions performed a signal service in educating for mission. Josiah Pratt launched the *Missionary Register* in 1813. It was noteworthy for thoughtful and thorough articles and field surveys that encompassed all Christian traditions actively engaged in mission. Pratt regularly featured statistical summaries of the number of work-ers, fields, church growth, and financial expenditures. He included all Christian traditions engaged in missionary sending, an early expression of ecumenical openness that became a hallmark of the modern mission movement. Other missionary journals and magazines followed Pratt's example. *The Missionary Review of the World*, founded in the United States in 1878, under Arthur T. Pierson's editorship, 1887–1911, filled this role for Protestant missions (Robert 2003, 156–61).

International mission conferences

Beginning with the Liverpool Missionary Conference in 1860, interna-tional missionary conferences stimulated in-depth studies and statisti-cal surveys of the progress of missions, which contributed significantly to the development of mission studies. These international conferences helped forge the style and substance of a missionary statesmanship that shaped the entire modern mission movement.

Yet these developments failed to attract academic notice and ac-ceptance. Henry Venn, a Cambridge University graduate and British mission leader during the mid-nineteenth century, repeatedly criticized the unwillingness of the universities to train men for missionary service (Shenk 1985). Although approaches and attitudes have differed among the various countries of Europe and North America, a common theme has been the persistent ambivalence of the academy toward missions and mission studies.

The first Protestant to qualify for a professorship in mission studies was Karl Graul (1814–64). He died before his installation as professor at Erlangen University was completed in 1864. In 1867 Alexander Duff (1806–78) was installed in the chair of evangelistic theology at New College, Edinburgh. This proved to be a short-lived experiment, in part because of Duff's failing health.

Twentieth-century breakthrough

The pace of the missionary movement began to quicken toward the end of the nineteenth century. The sources of new energy were multiple.

Students

The founding of the Student Volunteer Movement (SVM) in 1886, which over the next thirty-five years enlisted an estimated 20,000 men and women in North America and Europe in missionary service, fostered a closer working relationship between university-level education and missions. Outstanding SVM staff, such as Robert E. Speer, soon emerged as leaders of the major mission boards. Through his speaking and writing, Speer became a thought leader. Early in his career he began to advocate development of a "science of mission" (Speer 1902) and promoted progressive policies with regard to developing indigenous churches. Speer not only spoke out in behalf of mission studies, he produced an outpouring of articles, pamphlets, and books on a wide range of mission topics. Nonetheless, mission studies remained marginal to the academy.

Mission agencies

The Foreign Missions Conference of North America (FMC) was founded in 1893. FMC annual meetings brought together leaders of member mission boards to discuss a wide range of practical and theoretical issues in a spirit of fellowship and out of concern for faithfulness to Christ's mission. Both mainline and conservative Protestants were members of FMC.

Foothold in the academy

In 1896 Gustav Warneck, pioneer Protestant missiologist, was installed as professor of the science of missions at the University of Halle. In 1874 he had established the scholarly journal *Allgemeine Missionszeitschrift* and was a prodigious writer and researcher in the field of mission studies. Father Joseph Schmidlin, a professor of dogmatics and patrology at the University of Münster, was inspired by Warneck's work to develop a missiology based on the Catholic tradition. In 1910 the university gave Schmidlin a mission lectureship in missiology. In addition to lecturing, he wrote prolifically. His two major works were translated into English and published by Mission Press, SVD, at Techny, Illinois: *Catholic Mission Theory* (1931) and *Catholic Mission History* (1933). From the 1920s Catholics wishing to pursue a doctorate in missiology went to Rome (Dries 1998, 259–62).

Mission conferences

The Ecumenical Missions Conference held in New York in 1900 was a major event that attracted a record attendance for a mission conference. It put the spotlight on the growing world mission movement, encouraging a new generation of missions literature, especially curricula geared to laypeople in local congregations. That same year the Interdenominational Federation of Woman's Foreign Mission Boards launched the Central Committee for the United Study of Missions (CCUSM). CCUSM sponsored the publication of an annual mission study book as well as other mission literature for women. The Student Volunteer Movement and the Young People's Missionary Movement produced a variety of publications for students.

The World Missionary Conference at Edinburgh in 1910 promoted mission studies in several ways. Following Edinburgh the North American FMC was reorganized. The Missionary Research Library (MRL) was founded in 1914 in New York City with the ambitious goal of assembling the most complete mission reference library in the world. Emphasis was placed on gathering, interpreting, and disseminating information vital to the missionary enterprise. The FMC secured a professional staff and set in motion a program of missiological research and reflection. Annual meetings became strategy sessions where mission board executives, board members, missionaries, and professors of missions pooled information and insights.

At Edinburgh the decision was taken to found the *International Review of Missions (IRM)* starting in 1912. The *IRM* quickly became the premier missiological journal in the English language. The *IRM* was the symbol of the global mission movement and the means of maintaining a comprehensive perspective. A second decision taken at Edinburgh was to found the International Missionary Council (IMC). Following World War I the IMC was established in 1921 and under the leadership of J. H. Oldham, who had studied with Warneck in Germany, continually led the way in developing mission studies.

Growth of mission studies in North America

Prior to Edinburgh there were only four full missions professorships in the United States, at Omaha Theological Seminary (Presbyterian), Southern Baptist Theological Seminary, Episcopal Theological Seminary at Cambridge, and Yale Divinity School (WMC VI, 79–83, 173–77). Immediately after Edinburgh four additional professorships were established and the Kennedy School of Missions at the Hartford Seminary Foundation was set up to provide specialized missionary training (Myklebust 1957, 71). In 1917 the Fellowship of Professors of Missions of the Atlantic Seaboard (FPMAS) was organized. It sponsored semiannual meetings for the benefit of those teaching at the graduate level in the field of missions in seminaries and universities on the East Coast. The term *missiology* had not yet gained currency, and mission studies remained marginal in the theological curriculum.

R. Pierce Beaver observed, "The most intensive and high quality missiological discussion" in North America during the period 1920–60 took place in what was variously known as the Lux Mundi (LM) or *IRM* group. A. L. Warnhuis, North American secretary of the IMC, established the group in the early 1920s as an informal, off-the-record gathering of mission leaders who met for freewheeling discussion of vital issues. Mission historian Kenneth Scott Latourette was a longtime member. He regularly sought this group's counsel concerning themes and writers of articles for *International Review of Missions*. Latourette then passed these suggestions along to J. H. Oldham, *IRM* editor (Beaver 1979, 2; Latourette 1967, 76). "The genius of the group was that it brought together a select group of people deeply involved in leadership of the missions cause from their posts as denominational or mission agency executives and professors of missions" (Beaver 1979, 2). Its weakness was that it restricted membership. By the 1960s, as mainline Protestant missions were shrinking, LM began to decline rapidly and was formally dissolved in 1971. In important respects it was the conceptual prototype of the future American Society of Missiology.

Crisis in mission studies at midcentury

The immediate historical backdrop to the pervasive sense of crisis in the 1950s was the "closing" of China in 1949 and the expulsion of missionaries from that country. It was a low-water mark for missions—in sharp contrast to the mood symbolized by Edinburgh 1910.

Myklebust proposal

In 1951 senior European missiologist O. G. Myklebust, director of the Egede Institute of Missionary Study and Research in Oslo, Norway, published a proposal calling for the founding of an International Institute of Scientific Missionary Research that would (1) comprise "an international association of missiologists (and others engaged in the scholarly study of missions)," (2) convene periodic "international conferences for the discussion of missionary subjects in a strictly scientific spirit," and (3) sponsor publication of a "scholarly review of high standard" (Myklebust 1986, 4–11). American colleagues were consulted when the Myklebust proposal was first mooted, and they gave their warm endorsement. But this initiative failed to gain traction either in Europe or in North America.

Association of Professors of Missions

The founding of the Association of Professors of Missions (APM) in 1952, at Louisville, Kentucky, came in response to the deepening difficulties of mission studies in academic institutions. R. Pierce Beaver, doyen of mission studies in the United States during this period, later recalled that "new justification for the inclusion of missions in the seminary curriculum had to be found and the very existence of the discipline had to be defended. Our Association of Professors of Missions came into existence . . . not as an expression of the old missionary triumphalism but as an attempt to build a lifeboat for floundering brothers and sisters" (Horner 1987, 2). Mainline Protestant seminaries were now trying to curtail or eliminate mission courses.

The APM attempted to build on and extend the work of its predecessor, the Fellowship of Professors of Missions, which confined itself geographically to the East Coast. Following the precedent of the FPMAS, the APM received into membership only members of faculties of graduate schools in the United States and Canada—that is, institutions accredited by the American Association of Theological Schools (AATS). It was closed to those teaching at the collegiate level. Later this rule was amended to allow the executive committee to invite other people to join. The APM met biennially in conjunction with the AATS (Jackson 1967, 57; Lacy 1970, 39; Horner 1987).

Winds of change

The 1960s were a momentous decade for Roman Catholics. Vatican Council II issued decrees on mission that would reshape Catholic missions, and winds of change and challenge were sweeping through the missionary orders and seminaries. Catholic seminaries underwent major consolidation and retrenchment as the number of seminarians entered a period of decline (see Damboriena 1971, 73–87; Stransky 1982, 344).

In his presidential address to the American Historical Association in 1968, eminent Harvard Sinologist John King Fairbank made a provocative observation. He referred to the missionary as the "invisible" figure in American history and challenged his professional colleagues with the significance of the missionary movement from the United States for an adequate understanding of US expansion at the turn of the century (Fairbank 1969, 876–78). Fairbank was aware of untapped research riches stored in mission archives.[1] This awareness portended new possibilities for collaboration between professional missiologists and other academic disciplines.

The budding crisis in mission studies of the early 1950s came to full flower in the 1960s. This was a crisis of multiple dimensions for mission agencies, missionary training, and mission studies programs across the Western world.

In the summer of 1968, European missiologists convened a Consultation on Mission Studies at Selly Oak Colleges, Birmingham, United Kingdom. With good reason, R. Pierce Beaver in his paper gave a somber assessment of the state of mission studies in the United States. He observed that mission studies in the theological curriculum were

1 Fairbank asserted, "Mission history is a great and underused research laboratory for the comparative observation of cultural stimulus and response in both directions."

precarious, and he forecast a "rapid decline and even its elimination from most denominational seminaries" (Beaver 1968). In addition to the continuing decline or termination of mission programs in seminaries, respected institutions such as the Kennedy School of Missions at Hartford and the Missionary Research Library in New York were being closed.[2] He argued that the only reason missions got into the curriculum in the first place was because of student initiative and mission agency demand. Now neither students nor mission boards were requesting courses in missions, and the academic institutions were rapidly eliminating this offering from their curricula.

Beaver called for a new conceptualization of mission studies. He asserted that "a lively, vigorous, and influential Missiology required a dual base." Well aware of what enabled the birth of mission studies in North America in the 1890s and early 1900s, Beaver called for a revival of the partnership forged at the turn of the century: specially trained missiologists plus committed theologians, on the one hand, and mission board members and executives on the other. Each one needed the other. "Academic study without day to day participation in actual mission operations tends toward irrelevance and gets little attention from administrators. Administration without illumination by academic study may lack vision and be deprived of an important instrument necessary to self-judgment" (Beaver 1968). He lamented that among Protestants, Rufus Anderson (1796–1880) and Robert E. Speer (1867–1947) had no successors—that is, mission executives who contributed both missiological and administrative leadership. But Beaver's proposal was doomed so long as leaders in mission studies remained tied to the American Association of Theological Schools. His vision could be realized only by organizing an academically recognized professional society that would help lead the way.

Sunset or sunrise for mission studies?

Not all signs during the 1960s pointed to inevitable decline for mission studies. In 1965 President David Allan Hubbard invited the sixty-seven-

---

2 By 1976 MRL holdings had been disbanded as a separate entity and were merged with the general library of Union Theological Seminary, New York. Another sign of the crisis was the steady decline in missionaries sponsored by the mainline denominations (see Stowe 1969, 1–10).

year-old Donald McGavran to be founding dean of a new School of World Mission and Institute of Church Growth at Fuller Theological Seminary, Pasadena, California. Hubbard's goal was to create a dynamic center for research and the training of missionaries and missiologists. McGavran brought to the task more than thirty years of missionary experience in India and a strong commitment to assisting midcareer missionaries in getting retooled. He had an international reputation as an expert in church growth and a passion for *applied* missiology. McGavran insisted that this generation was witnessing the sunrise of a new era for the Christian mission, and it called for a refurbished missionary training. Other evangelical seminaries also inaugurated new missions training programs during this time. InterVarsity Christian Fellowship's triennial Student Missions Conference at Urbana, Illinois, was growing steadily.

Sine qua non: Accredited mission studies

Although President Hubbard took satisfaction in the strong start Dr. McGavran made in launching the School of World Mission, he recognized that the school could remain a part of the seminary only if the necessary steps were taken to establish missiology as a credible academic field of studies. McGavran was indifferent to this concern, and Hubbard turned to another faculty colleague who would play a leading role in achieving this goal over the next ten years: Ralph D. Winter. He had returned from ten years of missionary service in Guatemala in 1967 and joined the faculty of Fuller's new School of World Mission. For the next decade, Winter worked to complete the mandate Hubbard had given him.

Requirements for academic recognition

Hubbard outlined the steps that must be taken to establish missiology as an academically recognized field of study. To gain such recognition, said Hubbard, missiologists had to establish a professional society that (1) maintained a membership roster and met regularly, (2) published a peer-reviewed scholarly journal, and (3) promoted publication of monographs in the field of mission studies (Kraft 2005, 95; Shenk 2010, 92–93). No such professional society for mission studies had ever been organized in North America.

Laying the groundwork

In 1970 Winter attended the biennial meeting of the Association of Professors of Missions. He noted that only fourteen members, plus several guests, had registered for this meeting. Morale was palpably low. It was agreed that the APM executive committee should evaluate the purposes of the group and its membership requirements. Winter later recalled, "I immediately perceived an absence of the main bulk of mission teaching and research in the meeting." The reason was clear: "The original definition of membership excluded Bible colleges and other undergraduate schools where a host of active professors had been teaching hundreds of students for years" (Winter 1987; Horner 1987, 121).

Returning in the spring of 1970 from a decade of teaching in the Philippines to assume the presidency of Scarritt College for Christian Workers, Gerald H. Anderson also attended the June 16–18, 1970, APM meeting. "I was rather dismayed and astonished that only about fourteen persons showed up for that meeting. I was dismayed," he later remarked, "because I felt that if this represented the future of mission studies in the United States, then we were in very serious trouble" (Anderson 1987). Anderson and Winter discovered their common concern and started a conversation about the future of mission studies in North America and what might be done to provide leadership.

Finding a solution would not be easy. Some evangelical professors of missions were ambivalent about the APM. In 1965, in conjunction with the IVCF Urbana Convention, David J. Hesselgrave convened an exploratory meeting with a view to forming an Association of Evangelical Professors of Missions (AEPM) "in order to provide a forum for interaction between teachers of missions in our Bible schools, Christian colleges, and seminaries" (Hesselgrave 1983, 8–9; 1984, 65). The new organization, formed in 1968, was intended as an alternative to the APM. The AEPM did not find its footing immediately, however, and for a number of years it failed to draw members into active participation.

Myklebust proposal revived

After lying dormant for nearly two decades, the 1951 Myklebust proposal was finally revived and a group of European missiologists met in Oslo, Norway, in 1970 for the purpose of forming the International Association for Mission Studies (IAMS). Failing to achieve full agreement during the meeting, they agreed to postpone action temporarily. In 1972 the IAMS was organized at Driebergen, the Netherlands. Gerald H. Anderson was invited to represent the United States in the new IAMS executive committee. When the IAMS was finally formed, it was envisaged as an international umbrella under which would be organized a worldwide network of national or regional missiological associations (see Anderson 2012, 1–9).

Conclusion

These initiatives on both sides of the Atlantic boosted morale: mission studies were about to enter a phase of unprecedented development. In North America this would mean that mission studies finally gained academic legitimacy while training a new generation of missiologists and producing *instrumenta studiorum* that included encyclopedias, dictionaries, bibliographies, monographs, journals, and a rich offering of scholarly journal articles. The American Society of Missiology was to play a central role in these developments.

2

Founding the American Society of Missiology

During 1971 Ralph D. Winter and Gerald H. Anderson began laying the foundation for an academically recognized mission studies professional society. They envisaged an organization that would promote scholarly research, discussion, publication, and teaching in the field of mission studies. It would be open to a broad spectrum of people associated with the mission enterprise and would invite the participation of missiologists from all Christian traditions. Winter and Anderson recognized from the outset that they would need to proceed sensitively with various potential constituent groups.

Canvassing for support

Winter and Anderson agreed to a division of labor: Winter would contact the self-defined evangelicals, while Anderson would cultivate relationships with people connected to the National Council of Churches. Although Winter personally was a part of both the Association of Professors of Missions (APM) and the Division of Overseas Ministries of the National Council of Churches of Christ in the USA (NCCCUSA) in his past relationships and present ordination (Presbyterian), he was nevertheless invited to the large Greenlake consultation on "The Church and Her Mission" in 1971. This meeting was convened by the Evangelical Foreign Missions Association and brought together nearly 1,000 North American mission leaders and professors plus church leaders from other continents. Winter and George Peters, Dallas Theological Seminary, were permitted to convene a special meeting to discuss potential interest in an ASM-type organization. Sixty-five people attended and more than fifty agreed to join the organization, if it were founded, even though it was made clear that the new organization would include Roman Catholics. Winter subsequently reported this reassuring interest to Anderson, and they continued to make tentative plans.

In early 1972, Winter prepared a draft letter that was circulated to a select group of well-known missiologists for their counsel. On March 22 a revised letter was then sent to a larger group inviting them to meet June 9–10, 1972, on the campus of Scarritt College, Nashville, Tennessee, for the purpose of founding an American Society of Missiology. The APM was already scheduled to meet at Scarritt, June 12–14. The timing of the call to form a new missiological society seemed wrong to some people, especially several APM members. The APM had its own evaluation under way and expected to receive a report only two days after the ad hoc group was to meet. Assurances to the contrary, it appeared the initiative to found the ASM was calculated to put an end to the APM.[1]

Anderson and Winter had indeed concluded that the APM was a troubled organization with a limited future. They were convinced that what was needed was an enlarged vision that would call forth fresh energies and new resources. This required a new organization with flexibility to innovate. The APM had not proved to be an adequate structure to gain recognition as an academically accredited missiological society. Furthermore, Winter was concerned that the past polarization between APM and AEPM would doom the effort if it were carried out in the name of the APM (Anderson 1987; Winter 1984, 274–75; 1987). Nonetheless, Anderson and Winter made it clear that it was not their purpose to address the future of APM. That remained for APM members to decide.

Exploratory meeting

Forty-five people met in Nashville, June 9–10, 1972, to consider the Winter-Anderson proposal. Several points concerning membership were emphasized. First, the new organization was to be inclusive. Missiologists from all Christian traditions would be welcomed. The group hoped to attract scholars from a variety of academic disciplines in addition to the traditional field of mission studies. Furthermore, the new society

---

1 A representative counsel of caution was that of Per Hassing, Boston University School of Theology, and Donald M. Wodarz, St. John's Seminary, who wrote on behalf of the Boston Theological Institute, March 9, 1972, (1) saying they agreed that the kind of society Winter and Anderson proposed was needed, but (2) criticizing candidly the timing of the meeting and the "intemperate rush to judgment and decision" (Hassing and Wodarz 1972).

would be open to mission executives and missionaries as well as professional scholars. This synergy was deemed to be indispensable if mission studies were to be reinvigorated.

Second, the purpose was to found a professional scholarly society for mission studies recognized in the world of scholarly societies. In other words, it would meet the criteria President Hubbard outlined to Ralph Winter in 1967: dues-paying members that met annually, publication of a peer-reviewed journal, and sponsored publication of scholarly monographs. These visionaries saw an opportunity to develop a positive and robust identity for mission studies as an academic field of study.

Each of these points elicited debate. Not all professors were comfortable with the prospect of a society that admitted nonacademics into its ranks. Others, such as R. Pierce Beaver, who felt indebted to the old LM group, believed that the health and viability of the society depended on exactly this step. It was generally agreed that the proposed ASM should be a scholarly group, but shades of the old polarization between those of a practical bent and those committed to rigorous scholarship appeared. Many rejected altogether this dichotomy: effective praxis and rigorous reflection should go hand in hand. Should the new society define its purpose as that of fulfilling our Lord's final command or simply as the study of missiology without reference to doctrine? The nonconfessional stance was the only one likely to win acceptance among other academic disciplines. In the end, the latter position prevailed. Indeed, it was conservative evangelicals who asserted that they could join only if the new organization were *strictly scientific* (*ASM Newsletter*, January 1973, 1).

Scholarly journal

In 1972 no scholarly missiological journal was being published in North America. Most mission societies had their promotional magazines, and the Evangelical Foreign Missions Association and Interdenominational Foreign Mission Association were publishing the *Evangelical Missions Quarterly*, geared to the needs of their constituent agencies and their missionaries for applied missiology. During this time it also became known that *Practical Anthropology*, a journal that had met an important need among missionaries for nearly two decades, was about to cease publication. Adding to the concern for a mission journal was the rumored merger of the *International Review of Mission* with the *Ecumenical Review*, both published by the World Council of Churches.[2]

Although there was enthusiasm for an ASM-sponsored scholarly journal, the financial risks involved and the reported intention of the International Association for Mission Studies (IAMS) to publish a new international journal of mission studies caused some to hesitate. On the other hand, the majority felt that this was an important moment in which to focus energies and generate new momentum.

Draft proposal approved

In spite of some lingering suspicion and resentment over the way the proposal for the new society had been put forward, the Nashville meeting unanimously agreed to move ahead with formation of the American Society of Missiology. It was decided to hold an organizing meeting one year later. Meanwhile articles of incorporation would be drawn up and bylaws drafted. An announcement was circulated with an invitation to become founding members.

To further allay lingering fears, a statement was released: "The new organization is not intended to take over the functions of two existing groups with similar purposes: The Association of Professors of Missions and the more recent Association of Evangelical Professors of Missions. The presidents of both, James Pyke of Wesley Theological Seminary and J. Herbert Kane of Trinity Evangelical Divinity School, participated in the meeting and joined the ASM as Charter Members" (*ASM Newsletter*, January 1973). The APM meeting, June 12–14, 1972, received the report of its own study committee on the future of APM and decided to give its support to the proposed ASM, graciously voting a grant of $250 to assist ASM with start-up costs.

A fourfold statement of purpose for ASM was proposed:
- To relate studies in missiology to other scholarly disciplines;
- To promote fellowship and cooperation among individuals and institutions engaged in activities and studies related to missiology;
- To facilitate mutual assistance and exchange of information among those thus engaged;
- To encourage research and publication.

---

2 In the event, such a merger did not take place. Both journals continue to be published separately.

This statement was subsequently amplified somewhat and included in the constitution.

A continuation committee made up of Gerald H. Anderson, Ralph D. Winter, and Donald M. Wodarz, SSC, was authorized to follow through on behalf of the society in the interim until the next meeting. To maintain momentum as this initiative was being developed and members recruited, it was decided to institute an *ASM Newsletter*. J. Herbert Kane, John T. Boberg, SVD, and J. Walter Cason were the editors for the two issues that appeared in January and April 1973. The newsletter was discontinued when the ASM journal, *Missiology*, began publication.

Founding assembly

More than ninety people attended the inaugural meeting of ASM held at Concordia Seminary, Saint Louis, Missouri, June 8–10, 1973. Membership was reported to have surpassed 450. The draft articles of incorporation and bylaws were presented and adopted (see Appendix E).

In organizing the American Society of Missiology there were no immediate precedents to fall back on. Those who carried the main burden of working out suitable structures were guided by basic principles and values. Over the years these protocols have been refined, but in principle they have proved to be wise and durable.

3

First decade: 1973–82

Signposts

- *Contextuality* and *contextualization* concepts introduced by Shoki Coe, director, *Annual Report for the Fund for Theological Education* (1972)
- *A Theology of Liberation,* by Gustavo Gutierrez (1973)
- Lausanne I: The International Congress on World Evangelization (1974)
- *On Evangelization in the Modern World*, by Pope Paul VI (1975)
- *The Coming of the Third Church*, by Walbert Bühlmann (1976)
- *Christianity in Culture*, by Charles H. Kraft (1979)
- "Mission and Evangelism: An Ecumenical Affirmation," World Council of Churches position statement (1982)

The years 1965–82 were marked by far-reaching developments that shaped and reshaped the world Christian movement. The seminal Roman Catholic Vatican Council II concluded its work in 1965. The continuing decline in missionary forces among mainline Protestants in North America was offset by the founding in 1965 of the School of World Mission at Fuller Theological Seminary and Trinity Evangelical Divinity School's Mission and Evangelism Department. Asbury Seminary followed shortly with the E. Stanley Jones School of World Mission and Evangelism. Several Southern Baptist mission training programs grew substantially during these years. The new Catholic Theological Union in Chicago offered a strong program in mission studies. Major missiological events took place during these two decades: Congress on World Christian Mission (Wheaton, 1966); Congress on Evangelism (Berlin, 1966); Assembly of the World Council of Churches (Uppsala, 1968);

Mission Conference (Bangkok, 1971); International Congress on World Evangelization (Lausanne, 1974); Assembly of the World Council of Churches (Nairobi, 1975); World Conference on Mission and Evangelism (Melbourne, 1980); Consultation on World Evangelization (Pattaya, Thailand, 1980); Consultation on the Church in Response to Human Need (Wheaton, 1983). A compelling apostolic exhortation, *On Evangelization in the Modern World*, was published by Pope Paul VI in 1975. The lines of debate kept evolving as new themes—liberation theology, contextualization, the holistic gospel, the "shifting center of gravity," and globalization—emerged. This was the environment in which ASM was established for the purpose of encouraging and facilitating critical reflection on the nature, purpose, and goals of Christian mission.

Becoming a functioning organization

The founding assembly in 1973 requested that the continuation committee appointed in 1972 be constituted the first executive committee of the new organization. Thus, Gerald H. Anderson became the first ASM president; Donald M. Wodarz, vice president; and Ralph D. Winter, secretary-treasurer. Serving on the first board of directors were R. Pierce Beaver; John T. Boberg, SVD; E. Luther Copeland; William J. Danker; Arthur F. Glasser; Per Hassing; J. Herbert Kane; George W. Peters; and James H. Pyke. The president and vice president are elected for one-year terms. The secretary-treasurer and board members are elected to three-year terms. The bylaws called for the vice president to succeed to the presidency. After being elected as vice president, Donald Wodarz left for Rome to pursue graduate study. It was agreed to fill this vacancy by asking Gerald Anderson to continue as president for an additional year.

The bylaws provide for two boards to conduct the work of the society. The board of directors oversees the work of the society as a whole. The officers plus nine members elected to three-year terms constitute the board. Past presidents of the society become advisory members of the board, with voice but no vote. The board meets annually in conjunction with the society's annual meeting in June. Additional meetings may be called as needed.

The board of publications comprises sixteen members, elected to four-year terms, plus the ASM president and secretary-treasurer. The board elects a chair and recording secretary from its membership and is responsible to appoint a publisher and editors for the journal and monograph series.

ASM was now legally incorporated and had adopted bylaws, but policies and procedures remained to be worked out. As noted earlier, an organizing principle of the ASM was that it be inclusive of all Christian traditions. From the first meeting at Nashville, it appeared that participation fell naturally into three groups: Roman Catholic, mainline Protestant,[1] and independent/evangelical Protestant. To ensure that each stream would be regularly and faithfully represented in activities of the society, it was agreed that membership on the board of directors and board of publications would be tripartite and officers would be selected on a rotating basis from the three ecclesial streams.

Professors and researchers in the field of missiology constituted the largest group of members, but mission executives and missionaries have been well represented. Membership has stood at around 500 almost from the beginning.[2] More than a quarter of the members reside outside North America. At the time of founding, it was questioned whether Canadians would wish to be included in an "American" association. Senior Canadian missiologists such as Katharine B. Hockin insisted that this should not be an obstacle and that it was more important to develop a professional society that served the needs of the field than to be detained by such considerations.

In order to ensure a tripartite pattern in leadership—Roman Catholic, mainline Protestant, independent/evangelical Protestant—it was decided to add a second vice president. Each year a new second vice president is selected who then succeeds to first vice president the following year and finally to the presidency. Selection of this vice president is rotated among the three traditions so that in the persons of the president and two vice presidents the tripartite balance is maintained (see Appendix E, Bylaws Article V).

---

1 The designation "mainline Protestant" refers to members whose denomination belongs to the National Council of Churches or World Council of Churches.

2 For one or two years, figures of more than 600 members were reported, but this almost certainly included a sizable group who were delinquent in paying their dues and no longer wished to be members.

APM action

In 1974 the Association of Professors of Missions amended its constitution to hold annual rather than biennial meetings, "usually in conjunction with the American Society of Missiology." Since then APM has met annually immediately preceding the ASM annual meeting, devoting itself to the pedagogical task in relation to mission studies. This resulted in new vitality for APM.

Securing academic recognition

At the founding meeting in June 1973, the board of directors authorized Ralph Winter "to pursue the possibility of membership in the Council on the Study of Religion and association with the American Council of Learned Societies" (ASM Executive Committee, 1973). The CSR, later renamed Council of Societies for the Study of Religion (CSSR), was organized in 1968 in order to strengthen the position of professional societies within the academy concerned with the study of religion through research, publication, and teaching.

ASM president Louis J. Luzbetak, SVD, made a brief announcement in the January 1976 issue of *Missiology*: "We are happy to announce that at its meeting October 4, 1975 the Council on the Study of Religion voted to accept the American Society of Missiology as one of its constituent member societies, effective January 1, 1976." Luzbetak went on to comment: "This is a historic landmark: on this day 'missiology' becomes a fully recognized academic discipline in North America" (Luzbetak 1976, 11). The ASM now took its place alongside ten other academic societies devoted to the study of religion.

Given the ingrained diffidence that other disciplines had exhibited toward mission studies, the ASM could indeed take satisfaction that it had been admitted into membership in the CSR.[3] Affiliation with the American Council of Learned Societies was never pursued.

---

3 The timing of the ASM application seems to have been propitious. One of CSR's early concerns was the promotion of scholarly publication. A CSR task force submitted a report in 1972 titled *Scholarly Communication and Publication*, George W. McRae, editor. Chapter 6, "The Economics of Mini-publishing: New Hope for Strategic Dialogue," was a slightly revised version of Ralph D. Winter's article, "Mini-publishing: New Hope for Strategic Dialogue," first published in the *Occasional Bulletin from the Missionary Research Library* (1972). Referring to the William Carey Library Publishers, and their special short-run publications, McRae paid tribute to Winter's "remarkable

During ASM's first years, a driving concern was to exert leadership and develop the field of mission studies through fresh initiatives. At the 1974 annual meeting the board of directors encouraged the officers to solicit funds in order to create an endowed lectureship in conjunction with the annual meeting. Other ideas considered were an annual book award, a revolving fund for publications, and fellowships for advanced study. None of these suggestions came to fruition during the first three decades.

International Association for Mission Studies affiliation

As noted above, from its beginning ASM was keenly aware of its relationship with other societies. In 1974 ASM voted to affiliate with International Association for Mission Studies (IAMS) as a regional member and encouraged its members to join IAMS. Several ASM members attended the IAMS meeting at Frankfurt in August 1974, carrying with them an invitation to IAMS to hold its next meeting in the United States. The invitation was accepted and IAMS met at Maryknoll, New York, August 20–26, 1978. That year ASM did not meet separately, except to hold its annual business meeting.

Publications

Even before the exploratory meeting in Nashville in 1972, several people had given intense thought to the founding of a new missiological journal. One part of the vision was that the new journal be established on the valuable legacy of older publications. The Missionary Research Library's *Occasional Bulletin of Missionary Research* had been appearing with decreasing frequency. Negotiations were opened with its sponsors about incorporating the *Occasional Bulletin* into a new journal (ASM editorial board 1973 minutes). These hopes were never realized. *Practical Anthropology*, already scheduled to cease publication at the end of 1972, had a circulation of more than 3,000 subscriptions. It was deemed highly desirable that the *Practical Anthropology* tradition be incorporated into the new journal that was intended to serve the same constituency. ASM secretary-treasurer Ralph Winter negotiated the transfer of *Practi-*

---

achievements in publishing for the field of world mission." Such goodwill and respect were critical to gaining ASM membership in the CSR.

cal Anthropology assets to ASM and continued as business manager of the resulting new journal the first six years.

Missiology launched

The continuation committee secured the services of Alan R. Tippett, professor of anthropology at Fuller Theological Seminary, as founding editor of *Missiology: An International Review*. Fuller Theological Seminary provided an invaluable institutional base for the fledgling society by permitting Winter to manage the journal and granting Tippett a reduced teaching load in order to have time to serve as editor. In addition, FTS gave a grant of $4,000 per year to cover editorial assistance and office expenses over the first ten years. Even though the formal founding meeting would not take place until mid-June, it was decided to launch *Missiology* as starting with the January 1973 issue.[4] By 1974 the production schedule was regularized with new issues of *Missiology* published in January, April, July, and October. To maintain its link to *Practical Anthropology*, each issue of the first thirty-two volumes of *Missiology* carried the line on its masthead, "Continuing *Practical Anthropology*."

Introducing the inaugural issue of the journal, Gerald Anderson asserted: "This new journal is launched within the context of a new era in the Christian world mission." He noted that although we celebrate the emergence of the church worldwide yet the fact is that the number of those who have not named the name of Jesus Christ is greater in our day than when Jesus was on earth. Therefore, "this journal comes into being as an effort of the American Society of Missiology to provide more resources toward better understanding and effectiveness in the Christian world mission"(Anderson 1973). In addition to the institutional and financial support of Fuller Theological Seminary, seventeen other mission agencies and educational institutions gave one-time financial grants to support the publication of *Missiology* (*Missiology* 2, no. 2 [April 1974]: 262).

Alan Tippett, an Australian Methodist with twenty years of missionary service in Fiji and a recognized anthropologist, was an ideal choice to develop the new journal. He approached his work with the instincts of a pioneer. In his report to the editorial board—later board

---

4 See secretary-treasurer's note following the table of contents for the April 1973 issue.

of publications—for 1974 he concluded: "I have a firm conviction that the symbiosis of theology and anthropology in missiography is turning to syngenesis—something new is being born." Tippett's dream was to foster this "something new" through *Missiology* and the ASM.

Tippett carried the bulk of the editorial load alone. Fuller seminary provided some secretarial assistance, but Tippett worked without the benefit of a team of editorial associates. In addition, beginning with the second volume, his editorials took on the nature of full-scale articles. At the end of his three-year term, Tippett signaled his intention to retire.

Arthur F. Glasser succeeded Alan Tippett as editor of *Missiology*. Since Glasser was dean of Fuller's School of World Mission, it was mandatory that he have editorial assistance. Charles Mellis and then Faith Annette Sand served as editorial assistants. Simon Smith, SJ, became book review editor. Glasser continued the Tippett pattern of producing an extended editorial with each issue. Attempts were made to include notices and reports on important conferences and research projects in progress. After ASM decided not to publish proceedings of the annual meetings separately, Glasser ran the main addresses of the ASM and APM meetings in the October issue of *Missiology*, starting in 1979.

From the outset a primary concern of the board of publications was the financial viability of its undertakings. It was a boon to *Missiology* to have the help of two Fuller faculty, Winter and Tippett, in getting the journal launched. But by 1978 Fuller was asking that the ASM wean itself from this subsidy, and a four-year phase-out was instituted, to be completed by 1981. Originally, it was proposed to pick up this financial burden by allocating funds from the ASM general fund. Instead, subscription rates were adjusted to cover operating costs and retire a $4,000 deficit inherited from *Practical Anthropology*.

Monograph series

Initially, launching the society's journal was the highest priority, but the other priority, development of a scholarly monograph series, required laying the financial foundation. Publishing books required financial subsidies. Gerald Anderson took responsibility for raising funds by seeking grants from various mission agencies. The Southern Baptist Home Mission Board and Maryknoll Missions, among others, made substantial grants, and the fund grew to a total of $5,500 by the late 1970s.

Meanwhile a committee was appointed to explore possible publishing arrangements and develop a proposal. Charles R. Taber chaired this committee until 1977; William J. Danker then assumed leadership and moved this initiative forward.

After further exploration and testing, an agreement was worked out with Orbis Books in 1979 to publish the American Society of Missiology series. A grant of $3,000 from the publications fund was made to Orbis to assist with start-up costs. The first two titles appeared in 1980. By 1982 five titles had been published (see Appendix C).

International project: Documentation and bibliography

In August 1970 a group of scholars met in Oslo, Norway, to lay the foundation for IAMS. One of the concerns identified was the need for "bibliographic, documentary, and information services" (Roxburgh 2012, 135). Beginning with the founding meeting at Driebergen in 1972, each IAMS assembly has included "workshops on documentation and bibliography." This concern was to become one of the major activities of IAMS. If the new field of mission studies was to become firmly established, attention must be given to the empirical basis of the Christian mission. Indeed, the closing down of the Missionary Research Library in New York was still fresh in the minds of mission researchers. At the moment when new initiatives were under way to get mission studies established, it was critical that every effort be made to argue for collecting and preserving the documents that were essential if the history of the modern mission movement were to be studied scientifically (see Irvine 1976).

From its founding in 1912 the *International Review of Missions* included a bibliography of current literature. The Pontifical Missionary Library began publishing its *Bibliographia Missionaria* in 1935. There were many other specialist bibliographies, but it was recognized that a new approach was needed that was global in scope and gave access locally. Fifty-seven people met in Rome in 1980 to take up the challenge of conceptualizing the task ahead (Glasser 1980). It was fitting that Willi Henkel, OMI, hosted the event at the Pontifical Urbaniana University and Andrew F. Walls presided. Implementation of this project would prove to be a considerable undertaking because of what lay ahead in terms of rapidly changing technology. But Rome 1980 succeeded in creating awareness and momentum. It stamped DAB—documentation, archives, and bibliography—on the missiological consciousness. DAB became a permanent and major project of IAMS; its story has been admirably told by John Roxburgh (see Anderson 2012, 133–56). From the early stage, ASM members participated in DAB.

Annual meetings

American Society of Missiology meets annually the third week in June. Since its purpose is to serve the needs of members scattered widely across the North American continent, as well as members overseas, location of the annual meeting is an important consideration. During the first decade annual meetings were held in various parts of the United States in nine different institutions (see Appendix B). The planning for each subsequent annual meeting was led by the incoming president. The first action of the new president was to announce the theme for the next meeting and introduce the program committee. As will be discussed later, this pattern was modified in 2010. Reviewing annual meeting themes for the first decade (see Appendix B), one notes that the proceedings and debates in mission consultations and conferences sponsored by the three main ecclesial streams often became the basis for ASM meetings. The 1976 meeting theme, "American Missions in Bicentennial Perspective," recognized the 200th anniversary of the founding of the United States and some of the implications for mission. R. Pierce Beaver edited the proceedings, which were published as a substantial volume (Beaver 1977). A question that was being discussed in various settings was incorporated into the 1980 meeting theme: "World Evangelization Today: Convergence or Divergence?" It was recognized that longstanding differences marked the Roman Catholic, mainline Protestant, and evangelical Protestant streams. Yet interesting convergences could be discerned in current debates. ASM provided a forum where these issues could be explored together.

The Saturday evening banquet held following the society's annual meeting, climaxed by the presidential address, enhanced the spirit of conviviality. One of the most valued features of the annual meetings has been the opportunity these occasions afford for forming friendships and collegial cooperation with scholars in the field of mission studies from diverse ecclesial streams and institutions.

An early innovation associated with the ASM annual meeting was the creation of a travel pool as a means of equalizing travel costs. The registration fee includes an amount that is placed in the travel pool. The travel pool policy defines the criteria for eligibility and the formula for reimbursement on a pro rata basis to those requesting this assistance.

Conclusion

In its first ten years, the American Society of Missiology had become a viable organization. Annual meetings were well attended. *Missiology* was playing an important role in cultivating and publishing scholarly work in the field of mission studies. By 1982 the American Society of Missiology series had published its first five volumes. But a dynamic organization must be attuned to its environment and poised to adapt as changes occur. During its second decade, ASM would see further growth in the scope of its activities.

4

Second decade: 1983–92

Signposts

- *World Christian Encyclopedia*, edited by David Barrett (1982)
- Lausanne Consultation on the Church in Response to Human Need (Wheaton, 1983)
- *The Other Side of 1984: Questions for the Churches*, by Lesslie Newbigin (1983)
- *Constructing Local Theologies*, by Robert J. Schreiter (1985)
- *The Church and Cultures*, by Louis J. Luzbetak, SVD (1988)
- *Translating the Message: The Missionary Impact on Culture*, by Lamin Sanneh (1989)
- World Council of Churches conference: "Your Will be Done: Mission in Christ's Way" (San Antonio, 1989)
- *Proclaim Christ until He Comes: Calling the Whole Church to Take the Whole Gospel to the Whole World*; *Lausanne II: International Congress on World Evangelization* (Manila, 1989)
- *Redemptoris Missio: On the Permanent Validity of the Church's Missionary Mandate*, by Pope John Paul II (1990)
- *Transforming Mission: Paradigm Shifts in the Theology of Mission*, by David J. Bosch (1991)

Ever since *contextualization* was introduced into the missiological vocabulary by Shoki Coe in the 1972 Theological Education Fund annual report, it had continued to work its way into missiological thinking, writing, and debate. Contextualization had appeared in tandem with liberation theology. These concepts challenged the Eurocentrism of much of the scholarship that long informed mission thought and practice. Even the notion of Third World theologies could be threatening to Western missiologists.

Annual meetings

The themes of the annual meetings during this decade reflected the tumultuous world in which missionary witness had to be worked out: Third World theologies, urbanization, gospel bias toward the poor, spirituality, models of cooperation, forecasting the future, and the fall of the Iron Curtain that ended the bipolar world dominated by the clash between the Soviet Union and the United States.

One of ASM's distinguished senior mission historians, Samuel Hugh Moffett of Princeton Theological Seminary, president for 1986–87, led in planning the 1987 annual meeting around the theme "Forecasting the Future in World Mission." David Barrett, pioneer in missiometrics and editor of the landmark *World Christian Encyclopedia*, gave the keynote address in which he surveyed the rise and development of "futurology" over the past century. He observed that "forecasting has now become a major scientific profession with widespread applications and methods. . . . Forecasting in mission, as we are using the phrase, is not the same as prophecy, nor prediction, nor fortunetelling, nor foresight, nor prevision, nor clairvoyance, nor divining, nor soothsaying, nor horoscopy . . . nor crystal ball gazing. . . . As understood here [it] is a range of ways of looking at the future" (Barrett 1987, 436). Barrett then presented ten elements that made up his approach. "In all such forecasting, it is necessary to strike a balance between caution and exaggeration, conservatism and undue boldness of thought," he averred (ibid., 437).

Moffett began his presidential address with characteristic wit: "I am going to speak about the past. I am a historian. My name is Moffett, not prophet" (Moffett 1987, 473). He argued that "no part of the past is irrelevant to the future."

With the approaching celebration of the 500th anniversary of Christopher Columbus's first encounter with the Western hemisphere in 1492, attention was focused on the five centuries of European interaction with other continents, often at great detriment to indigenous peoples and cultures. Relentless historical change inevitably renders mission models and strategies obsolete and ineffective over time. All of this was grist for discussion and debate in annual ASM sessions.

Evaluation and response

Entering its second decade, ASM faced two concerns: its quarterly journal, *Missiology*, and promoting publication of scholarly monographs. How could the rising costs of producing *Missiology* be controlled while exploiting as fully as possible the space available in the journal? Arthur Glasser was concluding seven years as editor. In view of the workload involved, the evaluation committee recommended that a team of editors succeed Glasser. Ralph R. Covell was appointed editor and James A. Scherer and Robert J. Schreiter, CPPS, associate editors. The book review section was to be expanded, and the new review editor, Francis M. DuBose, energetically set about improving the system for generating book reviews. The journal format was redesigned so that the same number of pages could accommodate approximately twenty percent more material. Covell discontinued the article-length editorials of his predecessors and periodically arranged for a guest editor to prepare an issue on a special theme.

After a term, Francis DuBose retired and Norman E. Thomas became review editor, starting with the October 1985 issue of *Missiology*. Thomas had a vision for developing *Missiology* as a bibliographical resource. He introduced several new features. In addition to increasing the number of book reviews, each issue of *Missiology* included a list of "Books Received on Missiology," and as a service to teachers and librarians in Asia, Africa, and Latin America operating on limited budgets, recommendations of new books in two groups: "Essential"—and, when budget allowed—"Important." As will be reported in the next section, some of these developments represented a new stage of international collaboration with a view to providing the field of mission studies with better access to first-rate scholarly materials.

Bibliography project

The January 1986 *Missiology* carried an announcement of the launch of a new project: "Selected Annotated Bibliography of Missiology." This bibliography would emphasize the interdisciplinary character of missiology as well as the emerging majority of Christians outside the West. Norman Thomas, general editor, working with twenty subeditors, would produce this new bibliography in two formats. The first version would be published in *Missiology* over a period of five years; the second version would be a compilation of the twenty parts issued as a single volume in the American Theological Library Association (ATLA) series published by Scarecrow Press.[1] This project would be included in the global annotated bibliography being developed by the International Association for Mission Studies (IAMS) documentation, archives, and bibliography project.

January 5–10, 1987, IAMS sponsored a workshop in Paris on indexing. The ultimate goal was to make materials available as widely as possible. It was essential that a common system of indexing be established to facilitate exchange. Norman Thomas represented ASM at this meeting, which brought together representatives from at least fifteen research centers, and bibliographical services from Africa, Asia, Latin America, Europe, and North America.

The original goal—subsequently modified—of the ASM annotated bibliography project was to publish "a comprehensive, annotated bibliography of the 10,000 most important books published in the field of missiology, 1960–90, in European languages, including fifteen subject areas and five geographical areas." United Theological Seminary offered an annual subvention of $7,000, augmented by some private contributions, to allow for hiring student assistants and purchase of computer equipment required for the project.

American Society of Missiology series

Twelve new titles were added to the ASM series during the second decade. This included two of the bestselling books the series has published: David J. Bosch's *Transforming Mission* (1991) and Paul F. Knitter's *No Other Name?* (1985). The series was contributing fresh scholarship to mission history, contextualization theory, the religions, and mission spirituality.

Doctor of missiology

Although the doctor of missiology degree had been offered by several US graduate schools, the Association of Theological Schools (ATS) declined to accredit the degree even though ATS accredited other professional degrees. At the 1985 annual meeting, Paul E. Pierson, dean of Fuller's School of World Mission, appealed to ASM to speak in support of the

---

1 Norman E. Thomas, "Selected Annotated Bibliography of Missiology" (1986), and "The ASM Bibliography Project on Missiology" (1987).

degree. In response, ASM passed two resolutions.[2] In 1987 ATS approved the doctor of missiology degree.

Fellowship of Students of Missiology

In 1985 several ASM members who were pursuing graduate studies began to explore the formation of a fellowship of graduate students of missiology. The goal was to develop a network among these students who were working at the master's or doctoral level. The inaugural meeting of the Fellowship of Students of Missiology (FSM) was held in 1986 in conjunction with the ASM annual meeting. The FSM reported it had twenty-five charter members from six countries and eleven states. George R. Hunsberger, doctoral student at Princeton Theological Seminary, was elected as coordinator of the new group.

The changing of the guard

The year 1988 was a time of transition. After nine years of service as secretary-treasurer, Wilbert Shenk wished to step down. George Hunsberger was elected to that position. As chair of the board of publications, Joan Chatfield, MM, faced the task of securing editorial leadership for *Missiology*, an editorial committee for the ASM series, and a new publisher. In consultation with other officers, Chatfield sought leadership for these positions with a sense that these decisions represented a critical moment in the history of the ASM and gave a strategic opportunity to hand the mantle to new people.

---

2 The two resolutions are as follows: "(1) The American Society of Missiology will be celebrating its fifteenth birthday in 1987. In the interval it will be reviewing the implications of its steady growth in members within Roman Catholic, Conciliar Protestant and non-Conciliar Evangelical churches. It has witnessed the steady enlargement of mission training programs in the graduate schools of these churches. Furthermore, the interdisciplinary science of Missiology, which combines intercultural studies, anthropology, history, cross-cultural communications and theology, has been considerably enlarged and refined during this period and has been supported by the ASM quarterly journal: *Missiology: An International Review*. This journal has gained wide acceptance throughout the academic world since its inception in 1973. (2) At the 1985 annual meeting of this society it was agreed to petition the Association of Theological Schools to recognize the legitimacy and value of missiology as a field of learning in its own right. Furthermore, it requested that ATS accept the Doctorate of Missiology as worthy of its endorsement and inclusion within professional degrees" (ASM annual meeting, 1985, minute 9).

The new editorial team for *Missiology* included Darrell Whiteman, editor, and Stephen Bevans, SVD, and Ruth Tucker, associate editors. Norman Thomas, who had become the book review editor two years earlier, continued in that role. The editors devised work patterns that made the best use of the strengths of each one in their areas of expertise. They established a joint review process for submissions and grouped articles that addressed a common theme. This proved to be a highly efficient arrangement and they soon were six issues ahead.

The editors cultivated the historical link between *Practical Anthropology* and *Missiology* by continuing to feature articles that dealt with cross-cultural processes in Christian mission. They also continued the practice introduced by Ralph Covell, previous editor of *Missiology*, of including an abstract of each article's central argument. Every second year the April issue of *Missiology* carried a listing of current ASM members. Throughout this decade the October issue carried the main papers delivered at the previous ASM annual meeting.

Kenneth D. Gill became publisher in 1989. The new ASM series editorial committee comprised James Scherer, chair; Mary Motte, FMM; and Charles Taber. During the decade 1983–92 the ASM series added twelve monographs to the list (see Appendix C).

Continuity

The patterns and goals established in the early years of the society were largely maintained. Initiatives in publication—the journal *Missiology* and the ASM monograph series—continued to play a significant role in developing quality literature in the field of mission studies. The pattern of rotating leadership among the Roman Catholic, conciliar Protestant, and independent Protestant ecclesial streams made the society a hospitable environment for ecumenical relationships and pursuit of common witness. Whether in regard to officer and board service, editorial responsibilities, annual program leadership, or authorship of published materials, this threefold pattern ensured that the breadth of missionary experience and insight were maintained.

In addition, the commitment to attend to the variety of disciplines related to missiology as an interdisciplinary field was firm. By engaging the concerns of different missiological vocations—professors, mission agency administrators, missioners, students, pastors, etc.—the dialogue was always lively. In these several ways, ASM embodied the dynamism of missiology itself. Although missiology might be regarded as a discipline still in its adolescence when compared with other academic societies, it was nonetheless exhibiting growing maturity and stability as it fostered conversation across disciplines, vocations, and ecclesial streams.

During the second decade, ASM's structures and patterns had become well routinized. George Hunsberger, secretary-treasurer, 1988–97, began gathering the accumulated decisions and policies of the society and its board of publication. This compilation became the ASM manual of operations, providing a ready reference for officers, boards, and members. The manual was formally adopted in 1997.

Annual meeting venue

Nothing symbolized the sense of continuity and stability more than the venue for annual meetings. Having followed a peripatetic pattern for the first fifteen years, which involved finding a new location each year, annual meetings beginning in 1988 were held at Techny Towers, Techny, Illinois. The cordial welcome by Divine Word International (SVD), the efficiency and grace of the conference center staff, the ambience of the facility, and the reasonable charges all added up to a sense that the society's purposes were best served by returning there year after year. There was a caveat, however. The main auditorium and number of sleeping rooms had a maximum capacity of 150 people. This limit would soon be put to a test.

American Society of Missiology archives

In 1987 it was decided to make the Billy Graham Center Archives in Wheaton, Illinois, the permanent repository for the official ASM records.

5

Third decade: 1993–2002

Signposts

- *American Women in Mission: A Social History of Their Thought and Practice*, by Dana L. Robert (1996)
- *Missiological Education for the 21st Century*, edited by J. Dudley Woodberry et al. (1996)
- *The Missionary Movement in Christian History*, by Andrew F. Walls (1996)
- *Biographical Dictionary of Christian Missions*, edited by Gerald H. Anderson (1998)
- *The Missionary Movement in American Catholic History*, by Angelyn Dries, OSF (1998)
- *Missional Church: A Vision for the Sending of the Church in North America*, edited by Darrell L. Guder (1998)
- *Dictionary of Mission: Theology, History, Perspectives*, edited by Karl Müller, Theo Sundermeier, Stephen B. Bevans, and Richard Bliese (1999)
- *Evangelical Dictionary of World Missions*, edited by A. Scott Moreau et al. (2000)
- *World Christian Encyclopedia*, edited by David Barrett et al. (2nd ed., 2001, 2 vols.)
- *History of the World Christian Movement*, vol. 1: *Earliest Christianity to 1453*, by Dale T. Irvin and Scott W. Sunquist (2001)

In the 1980s a compelling new missiological current emerged. Lesslie Newbigin was a key figure in this movement. Starting with *The Other Side of 1984: Questions for the Churches* (1983), he wrote a series of books in which he assessed the "Christian" situation of the West and called the churches to awaken to the new reality. Newbigin's challenge attracted wide interest. Until his death in 1998, he focused on "mission to the West" as a new priority. The decline of Christian faith over the past two centuries in what had been the Christian heartland for a millennium posed fundamental missiological questions. Newbigin's questions for the churches were quickly understood to be consequential for all the churches of the West. No church was immune to this virus. During the 1990s the "Gospel and Our Culture" movement enlarged the missiological agenda. Missiology could no longer be limited to Asia, Africa, Latin America, and Oceania. The West urgently needed a fresh encounter with the gospel.

Taking stock

The 1995 American Society of Missiology annual meeting was planned jointly with the Association of Professors of Mission around the theme "taking stock" of the field of missiology. It served as a wake-up call. The larger-than-usual attendance was evidence that there was potential for growth if ASM conducted its work with greater responsiveness to the younger generation and scholars from cognate fields. The meeting attracted fifty to sixty more people than usual. Additional housing in nearby Oak Brook, Illinois, had to be found at the last minute to accommodate all the registrants. The signal was clear: there was growing interest in mission studies, but the program focus and format needed to be redesigned if the boundaries were to be enlarged. And if attendance at the annual meeting were to grow, a venue other than Techny Towers would have to be found.

This combined ASM/APM meeting was important for other reasons. The effort at a broad appraisal of the state of missiology by focusing on the key disciplines that are critical to it—biblical studies, history, social sciences, theology, and missional theory and practice—challenged members to keep before them the breadth and depth of solid missiological research and writing. The speakers emphasized the cutting-edge issues in their respective fields and the implications for missiological work. Members were reminded that they cannot do their work effectively unless they stay abreast of developments in the cognate disciplines.

The joint ASM/APM meeting also allowed participants to experience the potential of an integrated approach. A single annual meeting organized within the timeframe of the combined APM and ASM offered greater flexibility in planning program. It seemed appropriate to explore the question whether the advantages of a single structure might justify merging the two groups. Joining forces would allow each year's program to be a single expanded event, with space given within it for professors to continue to focus on pedagogical issues, which had always been APM's concern. It was envisaged that there would be other parallel special interest groups working on projects that might run for a period of several years. But some argued that the integrity of the APM agenda would be lost over time.

That watershed event did, however, set in motion thinking about the future on the part of ASM. At the conclusion of the 1995 meeting the board of directors appointed a task force on future directions for the ASM.[1] A report, with recommendations, was submitted to the 1997 meeting. This report called for the society to "continue conversation with the Association of Professors of Mission about ways of integrating the work of the two groups so as to ensure coordination and minimize administration." It also offered a series of other recommendations:

- Shift the focus of mission studies to the future, rather than the past.
- Highlight the kind of formation for mission that is required in emerging new situations.
- Structure annual meetings to provide for interest groups to form and meet; include the possibility of work groups dedicated to study of a particular topic that would remain intact until they completed their project.
- Provide opportunities for younger scholars to have their work critiqued by senior scholars.
- Cultivate the threefold diversity that was a part of the rationale at the founding of ASM: academic missiologists, administrators, and missioners.

A meeting format dominated by a few keynote speakers who tended to be senior missiologists was the source of mounting dissatisfaction. The lack of breakout sessions was especially frustrating and caused aspiring scholars to feel shut out. ASM needed to become a more hospitable environment, one that cultivated and encouraged those getting started

---

1 Task force members were William R. Burrows; Margaret Guider, OSF; George R. Hunsberger; Wilbert R. Shenk; Norman E. Thomas; and Rena Yocum.

in the field of mission studies. The Fellowship of Students of Missiology served student interests, but it did not meet the needs of a growing group of emerging postdoctoral scholars.

The board of directors received the task force report and passed it along to the annual business meeting for discussion. Minute 6 records: "The Task Force report was discussed at some length and additional suggestions made. . . . MSC to approve the report for implementation as guidelines" (ASM annual meeting, June 21, 1997). Despite the lively engagement of members with the recommendations, no enabling actions that would lead to implementation were taken. Some effort was made in planning the 1998 annual meeting to make a place in the schedule for work or study groups to be formed, but these did not take off. By the following year the annual meeting returned to the status quo.

The lack of constructive engagement and follow-through on the recommendations pointed to a fundamental flaw in the ASM organization. While the secretary-treasurer and editors of publications provided continuity within their spheres of responsibility, the board of directors operated from year to year. There was no provision for executive leadership charged with responsibility to guide the society in its work. No one was responsible to maintain a long-range view of the field of mission studies—helping ASM respond effectively and strategically to the unfolding future. But if ASM is to provide leadership in the field of missiology and mission studies, it must maintain a long-range view and ensure that the annual meeting is hospitable, stimulating, and challenging to its members.

The annual meetings of this period revealed two other dynamics. While the attendance at the annual meetings remained fairly constant through the third decade, running between 120 and 130 registrants, there was a growing presence of women, constituting 20–30 percent of total attendance. Whereas during the first decade only one woman served as president, during the second and third decades, 1983–2002, six women held this office. The second visible dynamic was a growing diversity in age. As many of the founders and early leaders of the society moved into retirement, the younger generations filled the ranks. This was an encouraging sign that missiology had a promising future.

Publications

Missiology

The pattern introduced when Whiteman, Bevans, and Tucker took over the editorial reins of *Missiology* in 1988 continued to work smoothly and efficiently. Throughout the 1990s an average of fifty manuscripts were submitted for consideration per year, of which about half were accepted for publication.

Darrell Whiteman also initiated a plan to provide free subscriptions to the journal for Third World theological institutions that could not afford them. ASM members were invited to contribute to a fund for this purpose.

Under Norman Thomas's leadership, and with strong support from editor Darrell Whiteman, the number of reviews in each issue of *Missiology* grew steadily. By the late 1990s more than 100 reviews were being published each year. The four issues July and October 1996 and January and April 1997 combined reached a high of 151 reviews. In addition, 495 notes on books and videos received were featured. *Missiology* had become the premier missiological journal for book reviews in the field. More than 300 reviewers contributed reviews during the 1990s.

In 1997 the American Theological Library Association (ATLA) informed ASM that its serials project had selected *Missiology* as one of fifty theological journals to be made available on the Internet. ASM was asked to provide $500 to cover the cost of getting permission from authors, but ATLA did the work. All articles published in *Practical Anthropology* and *Missiology* were to be uploaded. This was ASM's first venture into electronic publishing.

American Society of Missiology series

In the period 1993–2002 fifteen new titles were added to the American Society of Missiology series (published by Orbis Books) (see Appendix C). William Burrows, editorial director at Orbis Books, was a strong ally who worked closely with the ASM series editorial committee. The selection of manuscripts was a demanding task. Only one out of four manuscripts submitted was approved for publication. The criteria used in evaluating a manuscript included "the quality of missiological research; originality or distinctiveness of viewpoint or thesis; readability and clarity of style; constituency balance; and marketability in the view of Orbis Books" (1997 report to the ASM board of publications).

Even before launching the monograph series, the board was concerned that the program be managed prudently and that it achieve financial viability. Experience underscored how tenuous academic publishing was. Notwithstanding the careful evaluation that went into the selection of each manuscript, fewer than half of the books published earned enough to cover their costs. A few titles did exceptionally well and helped cover losses on books that did not sell in large numbers. The book that proved to be an outstanding publishing success was David J. Bosch's *Transforming Mission: Paradigm Shifts in Theology of Mission* (1991).

ASM dissertation series

As an academic society committed to encouraging and enabling young scholars to publish their work, ASM could not ignore the publication of doctoral dissertations. The subject cropped up regularly in ASM meetings from the early years. Publishers generally refused to consider publishing dissertations. Occasionally, the ASM series committee accepted for publication a manuscript based on a dissertation.

Yet it was generally agreed that dissertations of high quality ought to be made available. A few publishers were prepared to turn dissertations into published books. ASM publisher Ken Gill agreed to explore and negotiate with one such publisher, University Press of America (UPA). Gill brought a recommendation to the 1993 ASM board meeting that the ASM dissertation series be launched in association with UPA. The recommendation was adopted, and an editorial committee was established composed of Robert Schreiter, CPPS (chair); Dana Robert; and Gary McGee. The committee worked out remaining details with UPA and began to develop the parameters for their editorial decisions. UPA required an author to provide a camera-ready manuscript in UPA standard form and with an index. The author had to agree to purchase 100 copies of the published book.

The first volume in the series appeared in 1997. This was *Vernacular Christianity among the Mulia Dani: An Ethnography of Religious Belief among the Western Dani of Irian Jaya, Indonesia,* by ASM member Douglas Hayward, Biola University. A second volume was published in

1998: Michael Parker, *The Kingdom of Character: The Student Volunteer Movement for Foreign Missions (1886–1926)*. Parker was on the faculty of Nile Theological College of Khartoum, Sudan. The third release in this series was *Conversion, Identity and Power: The Impact of Christianity on Power Relationships and Social Exchanges* (1999), by A. Sue Russell (see Appendix D for the complete listing).

Bibliography project

As noted in the previous chapter, Norman Thomas had a larger project in mind when he introduced the "Selected Annotated Bibliography of Missiology" project in 1986. Consultation with colleagues from other continents had confirmed the need for an annotated bibliography that would track recent books in the field of missiology. After the January 1987 workshop in Paris on documentation, archives, and bibliography (DAB) sponsored by International Association for Mission Studies (IAMS), the ASM board of publications assumed responsibility for what became the bibliography project. Over the next fifteen years Norman Thomas and a team of area editors worked to bring this project to completion. It proved to be a moving target.[2] Repeatedly the plan had to be modified—enlarging the project and further delaying the date of completion.

In 1997 Thomas reported that a total of 12,500 records had been entered in the database. Already two-thirds of these entries had been proofread and corrected. It was projected that by 1998 the volume would be nearly ready to be submitted to Scarecrow Press for publication in 1999. It was anticipated that following publication in hard copy, the bibliography would be made available on CD-ROM and/or online in an electronically searchable format. These projections proved to be overly optimistic.

In June 2002 Norman Thomas submitted his final report to the board of publications as general editor of *International Mission Bibliography: 1960–2000* (attachment, ASM board of publications minutes, June 20, 2002, meeting). The manuscript was completed and in the hands of the publisher, with publication scheduled for 2003. "It is the

2 Indicative of the continually shifting situation is this report: Norman E. Thomas, "Projected Media in Mission Archives and Documentation," *Mission Studies* V-2, no. 10 (1988), 136–41.

fruition of a project begun in 1986, and enlarged in 1987 to include a team of 36 scholars as sub-editors, with entries in all European languages." In 2003, twelve years after the original date of publication, the manuscript was published in the ATLA bibliography series by Scarecrow Press. A CD version was also produced by ATLA.

The bibliography project was only one piece of IAMS's DAB. The entire initiative encountered one crisis after another as a consequence of rapidly changing technology, the challenges inherent in multilingual and multicultural projects, shifting goals, and changing personnel. The reader is encouraged to read John Roxburgh's account of DAB, 1970–2012 (see Anderson 2012, 133–56).

ASM website

Edward Schroeder compiled and produced several newsletters in the late 1980s and early 1990s as a response to appeals for a means of sharing news and initiatives among members. Subsequently, interest turned to e-mail and the World Wide Web. During this decade the promise of computer technology and Internet connectivity became a critical new area of exploration for missiologists. These developments offered missiologists efficient ways of staying in touch with each other throughout the year.

In 1997 the board of directors approved the development of an ASM website using arrangements facilitated through the Council of Societies for the Study of Religion (CSSR) office. It was anticipated that the site would provide general information about the society; facilitate online subscription and membership services; and offer a searchable index for articles and books reviewed in *Missiology* and *Practical Anthropology*, links to important sites for mission research, and a bulletin board for sharing important items of interest. This proposal went through several iterations before final arrangements were made. Desired results promised by technology proved elusive.

Electronic publications

In 1999 ASM president Dudley Woodberry appointed "The Electronic Publications Task Force . . . with a mandate to examine the broad issues of electronic publication that relate to the Society. . . Their work will also investigate a proposal for a CD-ROM/Internet Resource for missiological resources" (ASM board of directors, June 19, 1999, meeting, minute

5). In 2002 the task force resigned, recommending that this responsibility be lodged with the new ASM publisher.

Financial stability

The financial position of the society throughout its third decade required vigilance. Membership rose from just over 500 to more than 600, and subscriptions to *Missiology* remained at about 2,100 for a number of years. But both membership and subscriptions began to decline somewhat after 2000, reflecting a broader trend in all phases of publishing. The publisher and editor of *Missiology* took steps to maintain continuity in subscriptions and membership, and to make the journal available at a special discount to students. Advertising revenue was also important. Modest increases in subscription and membership rates were made twice in the period, mainly because of the rising costs of paper and printing the journal.

From the beginning the society depended on services and facilities provided by institutions and agencies that have also permitted their staff and faculty members to serve ASM. Members serve without reimbursement or honorarium. During the decade 1993–2002 the following institutions made important contributions to the work of the society: Western Theological Seminary (office of the secretary-treasurer), Asbury Theological Seminary (office of the editor of *Missiology*), United Theological Seminary (office of the *Missiology* book review editor and general editor of the bibliography project), and Princeton Theological Seminary (office of secretary-treasurer).

Other relationships

During this decade, partnerships with other societies and organizations remained important for the ASM. A close relationship continued with the APM, including annual meetings held back-to-back at a common site. Membership in IAMS was maintained, and from time to time major financial contributions were made to a scholarship fund enabling Third World members to attend the IAMS triennial meetings. ASM continued its affiliation with the Council of Societies for the Study of Religion.

Another form of partnership emerged during this period. The Presbyterian Church (USA) and then the United Methodist Church began convening meetings that brought together staff from the denomination-al global mission units and professors of mission from related seminaries and colleges. Occasionally, other groups such as the Academy of Evan-gelism and Theological Education have also held their annual meetings during this time. These groups have met prior to the start of the APM/ASM sessions. The ASM provided logistical support for setting up these meetings at Techny Towers.

6

Fourth decade: 2003–12

Signposts

- *Constants in Context: A Theology of Mission for Today*, by Stephen B. Bevans and Roger P. Schroeder (2004)
- *The Mission of God*, by Christopher J. H. Wright (2006)
- *Dictionary of Mission Theology*, edited by John Corrie (2007)
- *Global Dictionary of Theology*, edited by William A. Dyrness and Veli-Matti Kärkkäinen (2008)
- *Beyond Christendom: Globalization, African Migration, and the Transformation of the West*, by Jehu J. Hanciles (2008)
- *The Witness of God: The Trinity, Missio Dei, Karl Barth, and the Nature of Christian Community*, by John G. Flett (2010)
- *The Cape Town Commitment: A Confession of Faith and a Call to Action*, The Third Lausanne Congress on World Evangelization (2010)
- *History of the World Christian Movement*, vol. 2: *Modern Christianity from 1454 to 1800*, by Dale T. Irvin and Scott W. Sunquist (2012)

If missiology as a field of study was a late arrival on the academic scene, the theology of mission emerged even more recently. A convenient marker is the International Missionary Council (IMC) assembly held at Willingen, Germany, in 1952. At Willingen the theme was the theological basis of mission. Historically, all ecclesial streams had interpreted mission within an ecclesiocentric framework. The deliberations at Willingen challenged this ecclesiocentric conceptualization. Contemporary biblical and theological reflection called it into question.

Although this development was controversial in some quarters, a consensus soon emerged that the true origin and basis of mission is the triune God. The same theological shift was under way in Roman Catholic theology, as Vatican II documents show. Since 1990 seminal works have appeared that continue to reshape the way we think theologically and missiologically about *missio Dei* (mission of God or sending of God) as the foundation of mission; this reframing challenges us to work out the implications in the life and purpose of the people of God.

ASM members have participated actively in these developments since the 1980s, but this conceptual shift in mission theology was not addressed in an annual meeting until 2008. That year President Darrell Guder organized the program around the theme "Envisioning Apostolic Theology: As the Father Sends." Except for Bosch's *Transforming Mission* (1991) and Bevans and Schroeder's *Constants in Context* (2004), no monographs on this theme have been published in the ASM series.

A professional society exists to help its members enhance their competencies in that field. Missiologists look to their society to (1) promote research, writing, and publishing that expands and modifies knowledge in the field; (2) cultivate collegial exchange; (3) mentor newcomers to the field; and (4) improve the way mission studies are taught. ASM relies on four main means of reaching these goals: (1) meeting annually, (2) reading papers at annual meetings, (3) publishing the ASM series, and (4) publishing the ASM scholarly monograph series (previously ASM dissertation series). To remain vital, a scholarly society must regularly evaluate its effectiveness in meeting its goals.

During ASM's fourth decade considerable energy was devoted to reviewing, evaluating, and renewing ASM structures and program. These efforts centered on publications and the annual meeting.

Publications

From its founding in 1973, ASM made publications a priority. These four decades were a period of accelerating technological developments that altered all aspects of how information is shared. Changing technology has affected every aspect of our publications programs. In his report to the board of publications in 2007, ASM publisher William Burrows highlighted the increasingly precarious position of all forms of publications because of the changing economy of publishing and selling books: big-box retail outlets put pressure on booksellers; online book-sellers squeeze out bookshops, including campus booksellers; and new technology quickly supplants existing systems. Burrows observed, for example, that "no one knows where e-publishing is going and what effect it will have on traditional publishing. . . . Everyone wonders where the trends are going" (report to the ASM board of publications, June 14, 2007, meeting).

Missiology

The period 1988 to 2002 had been characterized by long tenures on the part of the *Missiology* editorial team. Norman Thomas served as *Missiology* review editor from 1986 to 1999, and Darrell Whiteman, Steven Bevans, and Ruth Tucker were the editors from 1988 to 2002. By contrast ASM's fourth decade was marked by more frequent turnover in editorial leadership. Capable successors were found, but length of service was shorter. In his editor's report for 2006, Terry Muck, editor of *Missiology*, drew attention to the growing crisis in the publication of scholarly journals generally. Some journals were being phased out; others were being taken over by publishers that specialized in producing journals for academic societies. Negotiations between ASM and SAGE Publications began in 2006. These negotiations eventuated in the decision that SAGE would become the publisher of *Missiology* beginning in 2013.

ASM dissertation series

The difficulties in working with University Press of America intensified over time. UPA was eventually sold to another publisher that was not interested in publishing dissertations. In 2006 arrangements were made with Wipf and Stock to become the publishers of this series under a new rubric, American Society of Missiology Monograph Series. Wipf and Stock agreed to publish a maximum of four volumes per year in this series. This proved to be a fine arrangement. Since 2007 sixteen volumes have been published by Pickwick Publications, an imprint of Wipf and Stock.

ASM series

Angelyn Dries chaired the series editorial committee from 1998 to 2011. Between 2003 and 2012 seventeen volumes—the largest number produced in any decade—were published. Since the launch of the series in 1980, a total of forty-nine volumes have been published (Appendix C). This achievement was possible because of the excellent working relationship between William Burrows, long-time managing editor of Orbis Books, and the ASM series editorial committee.

Electronic publishing

Beginning in the 1980s e-publishing was discussed regularly at annual meetings, but it proved to be an elusive goal. New possibilities would be suggested but when pursued seemingly vanished. Among the possibilities envisaged were producing CD versions of bibliographies, sharing dissertations, making out-of-print books available, circulating syllabi, and publishing e-journals. Such suggestions cropped up regularly in the minutes and reports of the publication board. From its initiation in 1997, the ASM website had operated independently of the board of publications. In 2005 George Hunsberger, webmaster of the ASM website, requested that he be relieved of this duty and the website placed under the e-publishing committee's responsibility.

In 2006 representatives from the board of directors, board of publication, and e-publishing committee met to develop a "Strategic Vision for ASM Electronic Resources."

Sheila Smith drafted a comprehensive report based on this consultation and its recommendations, which was presented to the ASM board of publications in June 2007. This report provided the needed framework for dealing with specific issues coming before the board in the future. Philip Huber, chair of the board of publications, reported to the 2010 ASM annual meeting that a new committee had been formed to "study the feasibility of a new e-publication journal in the area of missional church" that would be of particular relevance to those concerned with developing missional churches in Western culture (report to ASM annual meeting, June 19, 2010).

Annual meeting

The annual meeting has always played a critical role in the life of the American Society of Missiology. It is the public face of ASM. This is where people meet long-time colleagues and form new friendships based on shared interests. The annual meeting can also create disillusionment and alienation if it fails to be a place of welcome, fellowship, stimulation, and challenge.

In 2007 President Darrell Whiteman placed on the board of directors agenda this item: "Discussion about the Society." This led to a wide-ranging discussion based on observable trends in attendance, the age profile of participants, feedback from members, and sociocultural developments that are (re)shaping the future of academic societies. Why, it was asked, did the attempt a decade earlier to address these concerns fail? (ASM board of directors minutes, June 15, 2007, meeting). A strong consensus emerged that a fresh attempt must be made to reform and revitalize the annual meeting.

The following day Whiteman reported this discussion to the ASM annual meeting and invited response from the floor (report of the board of directors, ASM annual meeting, June 16, 2007). Members voiced strong support for the proposed initiative to address these concerns. William Burrows, president-designate for 2008–9, promised to make "the future of the ASM" a priority of his presidency. The board of directors meeting June 20, 2008, adopted this action: "That incoming President Bill Burrows be commissioned to convene an 'ASM Renewal/Strategic Planning Group' to work over the next two years to lead a discernment process for the society" (ASM board of directors minutes, June 20, 2008, meeting).

Renewal and strategic planning

William Burrows designed a two-year review and planning process. As a member of the ASM task force in 1995–97, whose recommendations for reform and revitalization came to naught, he knew that it was crucial that the board of directors participate fully in this initiative. In addition to ASM officers, a planning group representing various age and interest groups in the society constituted the team. Burrows convened the committee for its first meeting immediately following the 2009 annual meeting, June 21–22. The committee met for two days in June 2010—a day before and a day following the annual meeting. The final meeting was held October 8–9, 2010.

The committee was divided into five task teams: (1) membership survey (Robert Priest, Darrell Whiteman, Scott Hagley); (2) media and publications (Nelson Jennings, Miriam Adeney, Phil Huber); (3) developing the ASM and its annual meeting (Bill Burrows, Bonnie Sue Lewis, Arun Jones, Robert Hunt, William Gregory); (4) missiology as a discipline (Gary Simpson, Wilbert Shenk, David Fenrick, Darrell Guder, Steve Bevans, Roger Schroeder); and (5) identity, purpose, and constituencies (Ben Hartley, Doug Tzan, Greg Leffel, Robert Gallagher). Much of the work was carried out by these teams (see report of the ASM committee on renewal and strategic planning to ASM board of directors, October 8–9, 2010, meeting).

Task team 1 surveyed the membership, which enabled the team to develop a demographic profile of ASM members. This provided an empirical basis for planning. For example, the evolving demographics have wrought a substantial change in the distribution of members among the three ecclesial streams that ASM has been committed to serving. By 2010 membership was distributed as follows: 61 percent independent/evangelical Protestants, 32 percent conciliar Protestants, and 7 percent Catholics. The survey showed that women make up 13 percent of the membership and men constitute 87 percent. One implication of these findings is that the commitment ASM adopted at its founding to rotate board and officer responsibilities among the three streams will have to be reconsidered. A way must be devised to spread these duties around among the membership so that no one group is overburdened.

Task team 2 presented a considerable number of recommendations to the board of publications concerning priorities and needed actions. These were approved by that board and implementation began immediately.

Task team 3's key recommendation was that the annual meeting be restructured in strategic ways. These changes began to be implemented with the 2010 meeting. The critical change was to reduce the number of keynote addresses delivered in plenary sessions and shorten these sessions in order to make space for a series of miniseminars where volunteered papers could be presented and feedback given. This opened up the annual meeting to greatly increased participation.

The task team also presented to the board of directors a series of amendments that, if adopted, would incorporate these structural changes into the society's bylaws. For example, it was recommended that the first vice president be assigned the task of announcing and inviting proposals for papers six months in advance of the next annual meeting. Anyone wishing to present a paper was invited to submit a proposal. An ad hoc committee vetted these proposals. Those selected would be placed on the roster of the "volunteered papers" sessions of the annual meeting.

The task team called for an end to the "sovereign president" model of program planning. Instead, the board of directors was to assist the incoming "second vice president" to begin planning the meeting two years hence when this person would be president. This mandated a two-year planning process that entailed consultation with the board and other colleagues. Additional amendments to the bylaws were recommended that would update the ASM organization (see Appendix E). The result of this innovation has been enhanced participation. Beginning with the 2010 annual meeting attendance surged.

Task team 4, which was assigned to address the future of the field of missiology, proposed that a three-year critical reflection "on the enduring and changing tasks and practices of missiology" be carried out in three articulated stages. It recommended that the board of directors appoint a "continuation committee" to guide this process. A second recommendation proposed that a consultation be held in which "schools of theology that have significant PhD programs in missiology or closely related fields" would reflect on how they conceived their role in raising up the next generation of missiologists. This consultation was held the spring of 2011 and was hosted by Luther Seminary. The work proposed by this team is ongoing.

Task team 5 identified a series of themes that relate to ASM's identity, purpose, and constituencies. The first concern was to find ways of comparing ASM in 2010 with what was set forth at its founding in 1973. A series of issues was proposed to guide in that evaluation. Among the themes identified were the growing awareness that North America needs a fresh encounter with the gospel; the growing convergence between the three main ecclesial streams in their understanding of mission; the trend toward ASM becoming primarily a guild of academics, rather than including practitioners and administrators; and the decline in missionary anthropology represented in the shrinking number of anthropologists attending ASM.

A second area of discussion was the meaning of *American* in the ASM name and how this identity might be changing in the twenty-first century. The third theme was a call for an examination of ASM's identity and role in relation to other missiological societies: points of uniqueness, overlap, and complementarity. Should more attention be paid to potential collaboration in the future? The fourth query concerned ASM's present and future constituencies. It was recognized that there has been considerable development over the past forty years. We must align our understandings with present realities and plan for a future attuned to the emerging situation.

Council of Societies for the Study of Religion

The board of directors decided to end ASM's membership in the Council of Societies for the Study of Religion as of the end of 2004. This brought to a close twenty-nine years of association with the council and other academic societies in the field of religious studies (ASM board of directors minutes, June 6, 2004, meeting).

7

The unfinished task

The term *missiology* was not a commonplace in 1970 in North America. It had been used in Europe since the early 1900s, but the Anglo-American world preferred *mission studies*. More than semantic preferences lay behind this difference. Genuine differences of understanding and conviction were at play.

From the time of the pioneer German missiologist Gustav Warneck (1834–1910), Europeans were committed to pursuing mission studies according to the canons of scientific investigation and scholarship. Europeans regarded the Anglo-American approach as "nicht wissenschaftlich." Mission studies did not win a place in the British university until 1970 when a chair in missiology was established at the University of Birmingham. In North America virtually all professorships in the field were located in graduate seminaries rather than universities, and they emphasized the history of missions.

The decision to organize an American Society of *Missiology* in 1972 therefore signaled a shift of stance. The term quickly gained currency in North America and provided the field of mission studies with a new definition. The goal was not to adopt the European approach. European missiologists continued to adhere to the classical scientific model, with membership limited to those holding professorships in university faculties of divinity.

The ASM aimed to combine the Anglo-American pragmatic bias with rigorous academic research and writing. Over the past forty years the field has evolved and developed. A number of the newer mission studies programs, under the rubric of intercultural studies, seek to offer an academically rigorous training that equips people for effective ministry. This development reflects both a traditional cultural bias as well as the influence of the social sciences, especially applied anthropology, since the 1930s. ASM has never established formal criteria for membership. Rather it welcomes into its ranks those who have interest and experience in and commitment to the field of mission studies at the collegiate and graduate levels. It encourages people to join its ranks who are engaged in executive leadership in missionary organizations as well as mission-ers. This openness recalls the remarkable legacy of nineteenth- and early twentieth-century missioners and executives who made vital contribu-tions to mission thought and practice. This is a tradition that deserves to be cultivated and encouraged, as Professor R. Pierce Beaver, an ASM founder, never tired of reminding us. Professor Johannes Verkuyl em-phasized that "missiology may never be a substitute for action." Rather it functions like a "'service station' along the way" (Verkuyl 1978, 6). It must continually take in all kinds of data if it is to provide resources.

In its meetings and publications the ASM has devoted relatively little formal attention to clarification of the definition of missiology as a discipline. This is an important part of ASM's unfinished task. It is vital, therefore, that we recall an early statement of the task of mission studies, which remains as fresh and relevant today as when first written. Assaying the prospects for mission studies, James A. Scherer offered three sugges-tions for strengthening mission studies vis-à-vis theological education (Scherer 1971, 150–51). First, mission studies must be established on a firm foundation. The missiologist is not a disinterested observer but rather one who positively advocates. In a culture that insists that sci-entific objectivity demands detachment, this stance is suspect because it has an aura of subjectivity. Therefore, "its right to be present in the academic world will depend solely upon its competence." To maintain its place in this arena, missiology must cultivate an attitude of respectful attention and critical listening to other disciplines. It must courageously raise questions (see Montgomery 1986, 1999). Missiology must not be shy about employing all the tools available from cognate fields—anthro-pology, sociology, linguistics, communications, cultural theory, history, biblical studies, theology—to produce rigorous and insightful studies of the world. Careless scholarship is a disservice; missiologists must hold each other to the highest scholarly standards.

Second, missiology will keep itself relevant through constant revi-sion of theory that is informed by critical reflection on practice. In the popular mind the Christian mission has acquired an image of being dated and tied to the past. It is the mission of missiology to confront and interact with the entire range of theological and contextual issues of today and tomorrow rather than belabor the agenda of yesteryear.

Third, missiologists must be prepared to forge ahead even though the laurels of respectability are seldom tossed their way. "World missions reminds theology of the eschatological dimensions beyond church history and tradition. It recalls the church to her proper vocation of going beyond her own parochial life to be the witness and bearer of salvation to the world" (Scherer 1971, 150–51). This is a compelling call to be servant—a humble position, one for which in the short run the rewards may be meager. The challenge is to constantly refine the discipline of missiology so as to make it an ever more effective servant of mission.

The ASM was conceived to be a scholarly society dedicated to continual probing of the foundation of the Christian mission, its history across the centuries, and those practices that have proved to be effective as well as those that were counterproductive. The world is dynamic and continually changing. The task of missiological scholarship is to lead in critical study of this ever-changing world.

Over the past four decades ASM has contributed to this scholarly task by encouraging research, writing, publication, collegial exchange, and partnerships. This work has resulted in an ever-growing number of monographs and journal articles and other tools of scholarship. It has encouraged exchange with scholars from other continents. Annual meetings have become a place where new ideas can be tested through scholarly exchange.

Whatever the accomplishments during these forty years, the task remains unfinished. But looking back gives us every reason to be encouraged to move forward.

Appendix A

American Society of Missology officers, 1973–2013

Presidents

1973–74	Gerald H. Anderson
1974–75	Gerald H. Anderson (filling term of Donald M. Wodarz, SSC)
1975–76	Louis J. Luzbetak, SVD
1976–77	J. Herbert Kane
1977–78	Ralph D. Winter
1978–79	John T. Boberg, SVD
1979–80	M. Wendell Belew
1980–81	Charles W. Forman
1981–82	Joan Chatfield, MM
1982–83	Arthur F. Glasser
1983–84	W. Richey Hogg
1984–85	Janet C. Carroll, MM
1985–86	Charles R. Taber
1986–87	Samuel H. Moffett
1987–88	Joseph R. Lang, MM
1988–89	Alan Neely
1989–90	James A. Scherer
1990–91	Robert J. Schreiter, CPPS
1991–92	Lois McKinney
1992–93	H. McKennie Goodpasture
1993–94	Mary Motte, FMM
1994–95	Wilbert R. Shenk
1995–96	Dean S. Gilliland

1996–97   Angelyn Dries, OSF
1997–98   Jonathan J. Bonk
1998–99   J. Dudley Woodberry
1999–2000 Anne Reissner
2000–2001 James J. Stamoolis
2001–2   J. Samuel Escobar
2002–3   Margaret Eletta Guider, OSF
2003–4   William R. O'Brien
2004–5   George R. Hunsberger
2005–6   Stephen B. Bevans, SVD
2006–7   Darrell L. Whiteman
2007–8   Darrell L. Guder
2008–9   William R. Burrows
2009–10   Miriam Adeney
2010–11   Robert Gallagher
2011–12   Roger Schroeder, SVD
2012–13   Craig Van Gelder

Secretary-treasurers

1973–76   Ralph D. Winter
1976–79   Gerald H. Anderson
1979–88   Wilbert R. Shenk
1988–97   George R. Hunsberger
1997–2005 Darrell L. Guder
2005–2010 Arun W. Jones
2010–   W. Jay Moon

Board of publications[1] chairs

1974–77   Charles R. Taber
1977–79   James A. Bergquist
1979–82   R. Pierce Beaver
1982–85   H. McKennie Goodpasture
1986–92   Joan Chatfield, MM
1992–94   Charles R. Gailey
1994–97   William R. O'Brien

---

1 Note: ASM editorial board, 1973–79.

1997–98   Rena M. Yocum
1998–99   Margaret Eletta Guider, OSF
1999–2002 Roger Schroeder, SVD
2002–3   Brian Stelk
2004–6   Stan W. Nussbaum
2007–8   J. Nelson Jennings
2008–12   Phil Huber
2012–   Arun Jones and William Gregory

Publishers

1978–89   Willard E. Roth
1989–2002 Kenneth D. Gill
2002–7   William R. Burrows
2008–   Darrell L. Whiteman

Editors of *Missiology: An International Review*

1973–75   Alan R. Tippett
1975–82   Arthur F. Glasser
1982–88   Ralph R. Covell
1989–2002 Darrell L. Whiteman
2002–7   Terry C. Muck
2008–11   J. Nelson Jennings
2011–   Richard L. Starcher

Associate editors of *Missiology*

1982–88   Robert J. Schreiter, CPPS
1982–88   James A. Scherer
1988–2002 Stephen B. Bevans, SVD
1988–2002 Ruth A. Tucker
2002–8   Angelyn Dries, OSF
2002–6   Graham Walker
2006–8   Dale Walker
2008–   Jay Moon
2008–   Colleen Mallon, OP
2010–   Jehu J. Hanciles
2011–   Eloise Meneses
2012–   William Gregory

Book review editors, *Missiology*

1975–82	Simon Smith, SJ
1982–85	Francis M. DuBose
1985–99	Norman E. Thomas
1999–2002	Paul Hertig
2002–3	Terry C. Muck
2004–6	Robert Danielson
2007–12	Charles Farhadian
2012–	David Fenrick

ASM series editorial committee

1978–88	William J. Danker, chair
1979–88	Gerald H. Anderson
1979–88	Joan Chatfield, MM
1983–97	Mary Motte, FMM
1988–98	James A. Scherer, chair
1988–97	Charles R. Taber
1997–2011	Angelyn Dries, OSF, chair
1997–	Scott W. Sunquist
1997–	Jonathan J. Bonk
2011–	William R. Burrows, chair

ASM dissertation/monograph series editorial committee

1994–99	Robert J. Schreiter, chair
1994–2006	Gary B. McGee, chair, 1999–2006
1994–2007	Dana L. Robert
1999–2007	Anthony Gittins, CSSp
2007–	Michael Rynkiewich, chair, 2007–12
2007–	Paul V. Kollman
2007–	James R. Krabill, chair, 2012–
2007–	Judith Lingenfelter
2007–	Wilbur Stone
2009–	Richard Jones
2009–	Bonnie Sue Lewis
2009–	Roger Schroeder, SVD
2011–	Gary Simpson

Appendix B

American Society of Missiology annual meeting themes, venues, and presidents

year	theme	venue	presiding
1973	Salvation today	St. Louis, MO	Gerald H. Anderson
1974	Communication (no theme specified)	Wheaton, IL	Gerald H. Anderson
1975	Missiological implications of Lausanne—Rome–Nairobi	Dubuque, IA	Gerald H. Anderson (for Donald M. Wodarz, SSC)
1976	American missions in bicentennial perspective	Deerfield, IL	Louis J. Luzbetak, SVD
1977	Christ, salvation and the world's religions	North Park, IL	J. Herbert Kane
1978	Credibility and spirituality in mission (Joint Meeting with IAMS)	Maryknoll, NY	Ralph D. Winter
1979	For God's pluralistic world—An ultimate gospel	Techny, IL	John T. Boberg, SVD
1980	World evangelization today: Convergence or divergence?	Wheaton, IL	M. Wendell Belew
1981	Problems of church and state: The churches' common witness	Ft. Worth, TX	Charles W. Forman
1982	Emerging agendas in world mission	Evanston, IL	Joan Chatfield, MM
1983	Spirituality for mission	Wheaton, IL	Arthur F. Glasser
1984	Third World theologies and the mission of the church	Princeton, NJ	W. Richey Hogg
1985	Urbanization as a mission challenge	Deerfield, IL	Janet C. Carroll, MM
1986	Vital Signs of the Church	North Park, IL	Charles R. Taber
1987	Forecasting the future in world mission	Pittsburgh, PA	Samuel H. Moffett

year	theme	venue	presiding
1988	The Holy Spirit and mission	Techny, IL	Joseph R. Lang, MM
1989	Good news for the poor?	Techny, IL	Alan Neely
1990	Mission and joint witness: Basis and models of cooperation	Techny, IL	James A. Scherer
1991	Missionaries in situations of conflict and violence	Techny, IL	Robert J. Schreiter, CPPS
1992	1492–2092: Shifting paradigms in mission	Techny, IL	Lois McKinney
1993	North America—Peoples and their cultures in transition: Toward a missiology for a new era	Techny, IL	H. McKennie Goodpasture
1994	Images of church—Images of mission	Techny, IL	Mary Motte, FMM
1995	Mission studies: Taking stock, charting the course (joint meeting with APM)	Techny, IL	Wilbert R. Shenk
1996	Contextualization: Witness and reflection	Techny, IL	Dean S. Gilliland
1997	Marginalization and mission	Techny, IL	Angeln Dries, OSF
1998	Tools of the trade: Missiological reference for church, academy, and missionary	Techny, IL	Jonathan J. Bonk
1999	The new millennium and the emerging religious encounters	Techny, IL	J. Dudley Woodberry
2000	Creative partnerships for mission in the twenty-first century	Techny, IL	Anne Reissner
2001	Missionaries for the twenty-first century: Their recruitment and training, ministries and roles, care and nutrition	Techny, IL	James J. Stamoolis
2002	Migration: Challenge and avenue for Christian mission	Techny, IL	J. Samuel Escobar
2003	Racial justice and Christian mission: Redressing the counterwitness of racism—a missionary imperative for the 21st century	Techny, IL	Margaret Eletta Guider, OSF
2004	Collaboration: The missing link in the world Christian mission	Techny, IL	William R. O'Brien

year	theme	venue	presiding
2005	The mission of public theology	Techny, IL	George R. Hunsberger
2006	From Azusa Street to the ends of the earth	Techny, IL	Stephen B. Bevans, SVD
2007	Training for cross-cultural mission	Techny, IL	Darrell L. Whiteman
2008	Envisioning apostolic theology: As the Father sends	Techny, IL	Darrell L. Guder
2009	Emerging churches and other new Christian movements in North America: The challenge to missiology	Techny, IL	William R. Burrows
2010	Colorful initiatives: North American cultures in mission	Techny, IL	Miriam Adeney
2011	Mission spirituality in global perspective	Techny, IL	Robert L. Gallagher
2012	Prophetic dialogue: Practice and theology	Techny, IL	Roger Schroeder, SVD

Appendix C

American Society of Missiology series
(published by Orbis Books)

1. Everett Nicholls Hunt. *Protestant Pioneers in Korea.*1980.

2. Eric O. Hanson. *Catholic Politics in China and Korea.* 1980.

3. James M. Phillips. *From the Rising of the Sun: Christians and Society in Contemporary Japan.* 1981.

4. Eugene Nida and William Reyburn. *Meaning across Cultures: A Study in Bible Translation.* 1981.

5. Charles W. Forman. *Island Churches of the Pacific: Emergence in the Twentieth Century.* 1982.

6. Wilbert R. Shenk. *Henry Venn—Missionary Statesman.* 1983.

7. Paul F. Knitter. *No Other Name? A Critical Survey of Christian Attitudes toward the World Religions.* 1985.

8. Richard Drummond. *Toward a New Age in Christian Theology.* 1985.

9. Guillermo Cook. *The Expectations of the Poor: Latin American Basic Ecclesial Communities in Protestant Perspective.* 1985.

10. James Stamoolis. *Eastern Orthodox Mission Theology Today.* 1986.

11. Ralph R. Covell. *Confucius, the Buddha, and Christ.* 1986.

12. Louis J. Luzbetak, SVD. *The Church and Cultures: New Perspectives in Missiological Anthropology.* 1988.

13. Lamin Sanneh. *Translating the Message: The Missionary Impact on Culture.* 1989.

14. Thomas G. Christensen. *An African Tree of Life.* 1990.

15. Jonathan Bonk. *Missions and Money.* 1991.

16. David J. Bosch. *Transforming Mission: Paradigm Shifts in Mission Theology.* 1991.

17. Anthony J. Gittins. *Bread for the Journey.* 1991.
18. Guillermo Cook, ed. *New Faces of the Church in Latin America.* 1994.
19. Gerald H. Anderson, Robert T. Coote, Norman A. Horner, and James M. Phillips, eds. *Mission Legacies.* 1994.
20. Norman E. Thomas, ed. *Classic Texts in Mission and World Christianity.* 1995.
21. Alan Neely. *Christian Mission: A Case Study Approach.* 1995.
22. Marguerite G. Kraft. *Understanding Spiritual Power: A Forgotten Dimension of Cross Cultural Mission and Ministry.* 1995.
23. J. Dudley Woodberry, Charles E. Van Engen, and Edgar J. Elliston, eds. *Missiological Education for the 21st Century.* 1996.
24. Karl Müller, Theo Sundermeier, Stephen B. Bevans, SVD, and Richard H. Bliese, eds. *Dictionary of Mission Theology, History, Perspectives.* 1997.
25. G. Thompson Brown. *Earthen Vessels and Transcendent Power: American Presbyterians in China, 1837–1952.* 1997.
26. Angelyn Dries, OSF. *The Missionary Movement in American Catholic History, 1820–1980.* 1998.
27. William J. Larkin, Jr., and Joel F. Williams. *Heaven-Sent: An Evangelical Approach to Mission in the New Testament.* 1998.
28. Wilbert R. Shenk, *Changing Frontiers of Mission.* 1999.
29. Ernest Brandewie. *In the Light of the Word: Divine Word Missionaries of North America.* 2000.
30. Stephen B. Bevans, SVD, and Roger P. Schroeder, SVD. *Constants in Context: Theology for Mission Today.* 2004.
31. J. Samuel Escobar. *Changing Tides: Latin America and World Mission Today.* 2002.
32. Dana L. Robert, ed. *Gospel Bearers, Gender Barriers: Missionary Women in the Twentieth Century.* 2002.
33. John Fuellenbach, SVD. *Church: Community for the Kingdom.* 2002.
34. Robert L. Gallagher and Paul Hertig, eds. *Mission in Acts: Ancient Narratives for a Postmodern Context.* 2004.
35. Samuel Hugh Moffett. *A History of Christianity in Asia.* Volume 1: *Beginnings to 1500.* 1998.

Appendix C | 69

36. Samuel Hugh Moffett. *A History of Christianity in Asia*. Volume 2: *1500–1900*. 2005.
37. Stan Nussbaum. *A Reader's Guide to* Transforming Mission. 2005.
38. Paul Vincent Kollman, CSC. *The Evangelization of Slaves and Catholic Origins in Eastern Africa*. 2005.
39. James Chukwuma Okoye, CSSp. *Israel and the Nations: A Mission Theology of the Old Testament*. 2006.
40. Susan Smith. *Women in Mission: From the New Testament to Today*. 2007.
41. Philip L. Wickeri. *Reconstructing Christianity in China: K. H. Ting and the Chinese Church*. 2007.
42. Lamin Sanneh. *Translating the Message: The Missionary Impact on Culture* (2nd ed.). 2009.
43. Robert L. Gallagher and Paul Hertig, eds. *Landmark Essays in Mission and World Christianity*. 2009.
44. Darrell L. Whiteman and Gerald H. Anderson, eds. *The World Mission in the Wesleyan Spirit*. 2009.
45. Gary B. McGee. *Miracles, Missions and American Pentecostalism*. 2010.
46. Robert A. Hunt, ed. *The Gospel among the Nations: Christian Mission in a Pluralistic World*. 2010.
47. Norman E. Thomas. *Mission and Unity: Lessons from History, 1792–2010*. 2010.
48. Stephen B. Bevans, ed. *Mission and Culture: The Louis J. Luzbetak Lectures*. 2012.
49. Stanley H. Skreslet. *Comprehending Mission: The Questions, Methods, Themes, Problems, and Prospects of Missiology*. 2012.

Appendix D

American Society of Missiology Monograph Series

(1997–2005 ASM dissertation series, published by University Press of America)

1. Douglas James Hayward. *Vernacular Christianity among the Mulia Dani: An Ethnography of Religious Belief among the Western Dani of Irian Jaya, Indonesia.* 1997.
2. Michael Parker. *The Kingdom of Character: The Student Volunteer Movement for Foreign Missions (1886–1926).* 1998.
3. A. Sue Russell. *Conversion, Identity and Power: The Impact of Christianity on Power Relationships and Social Exchanges.* 1999.
4. Kevin Xihi Yao. *The Fundamentalist Movement among Protestant Missionaries in China, 1920–1937.* 2003.
5. George F. Pickens. *African Christian God-Talk: Matthew Ajuoga's Johera Narrative.* 2004.
6. Ross Langmead. *The Word Made Flesh: Towards an Incarnational Missiology.* 2004.
7. J. Nelson Jennings. *Theology in Japan: Takakura Kokutaro (1885–1934).* 2005.

(2007–13 American Society of Missiology Monograph Series, published by Pickwick Publications, an imprint of Wipf and Stock)

1. Ken Christoph Miyamoto. *God's Mission in Asia: A Comparative and Contextual Study of This-Worldly Holiness and the Theology of Missio Dei in M. M. Thomas and C. S. Song.* 2007.

2. Edley J. Moodley. *Shembe, Ancestors and Christ: A Christological Inquiry with Missiological Implications.* 2008.
3. Roberta R. King. *Pathways in Christian Music Communication: The Case of the Senufo of Côte d'Ivoire.* 2009.
4. W. Jay Moon. *African Proverbs Reveal Christianity in Culture: A Narrative Portrayal of Builsa Proverbs, Contextualizing Christianity in Ghana.* 2009.
5. Auli Vähäkangas. *Christian Couples Coping with Childlessness: Narratives from Machame, Kilimanjaro.* 2009.
6. E. Paul Balisky. *Wolaitta Evangelists: A Study in Religious Innovation in Southern Ethiopia, 1937–1975.* 2009.
7. David Endres. *American Crusade: Catholic Youth in the World Mission Movement from World War 1 through Vatican II.* 2010.
8. Colleen M. Mallon. *Traditioning Disciples: The Contributions of Cultural Anthropology to Ecclesial Identity.* 2011.
9. Chris Flanders. *About Face: Reorienting Thai Face for Soteriology and Mission.* 2011.
10. Steve Pavey. *Theologies of Power and Crisis: Envisioning/Embodying Christianity in Hong Kong.* 2011.
11. Shawn B. Redford. *Missiological Hermeneutics: Biblical Interpretation for the Global Church.* 2012.
12. David Leong. *Street Signs: Toward a Missional Theology of Urban Cultural Engagement.* 2012.
13. Ethan Christofferson. *Negotiating Identity: Exploring Tensions between Being Hakka and Being Christian in Northwestern Taiwan.* 2012.
14. Van Thanh Nguyen. *Peter and Cornelius: A Story of Conversion and Mission.* 2012.
15. Gregg Okesson. *Re-Imaging Modernity: A Contextualized Theological Study of Conversion and Mission.* 2012.
16. Jukka Antero Kääriäinen. *Mission Shaped by Promise: Lutheran Missiology Confronts the Challenge of Religious Pluralism.* 2012.

Appendix E

Articles of Incorporation
of American Society of Missiology, Inc.

I

The name of this corporation shall be AMERICAN SOCIETY OF MISSIOLOGY, Inc.

II

The purposes for which this corporation is formed are:

(a) The specific and primary purposes are to promote the scholarly study of theological, historical, social and practical questions relating to the missionary dimension of the Christian Church; to relate studies in missiology to the other scholarly disciplines; to promote fellowship and cooperation among individuals and institutions engaged in activities and studies related to missiology; to facilitate mutual assistance and exchange of information among those thus engaged; and to encourage research and publication in the study of Christian missions.

(b) The general purposes and powers are to have and to exercise all rights and powers conferred on nonprofit corporations under the laws of California, including the power to contract, rent, buy or sell personal or real property, provided, however, that this corporation shall not, except to an insubstantial degree, engage in any activities or exercise any powers that are not in furtherance of the primary purposes of this corporation.

(c) No substantial part of the activities of this corporation shall consist of carrying on propaganda, or otherwise attempting to influence legislation, and the corporation shall not participate or intervene in any political campaign (including the publishing or distribution of statements) on behalf of any candidate for public office.

III

This corporation is organized pursuant to the General Nonprofit Corporation Law of the State of California. This corporation does not contemplate pecuniary gain or profit to the members thereof and it is organized for nonprofit purposes.

IV

The principal office for the transaction of the business of this corporation is located in the County of Los Angeles, State of California.

V

The names and addresses of the persons who are to act in the capacity of directors until the selection of their successors are:
GERALD H. ANDERSON, 114 Catherine Street, Ithaca, NY 14850
DONALD M. WODARZ, Saint Columban's Seminary, 1200 Brush Hill Road, Milton, MA 01286
RALPH D. WINTER, 533 Hermosa Street, South Pasadena, CA 91030

VI

The authorized number and qualifications of members of the corporation, the different classes of membership, if any, the property, voting and other rights and privileges of members, and their liability to dues and assessments and the method of collection thereof, shall be as set forth in the bylaws.

VII

The property of this corporation is irrevocably dedicated to charitable purposes and no part of the net income or assets of this corporation shall ever inure to the benefit of any director, officer or member thereof or the benefit of any private persons. Upon the dissolution or winding up of the corporation, its assets remaining after payment, or provision for payment, of all debts and liabilities of this corporation shall be distributed to a non-profit fund, foundation or corporation which is organized and operated exclusively for charitable purposes and which has established its tax exempt status under Section 501 (c) (3) of the Internal Revenue Code.

If this corporation holds any assets in trust, or the corporation is formed for charitable purposes, such assets shall be disposed of in such manner as may be directed by decree of the superior court of the county in which the corporation has its principal office, upon petition therefore by the Attorney General or by any person concerned in the liquidation, in a proceeding to which the Attorney General is a party.

VIII

The name of the unincorporated association which is being incorporated is AMERICAN SOCIETY OF MISSIOLOGY.

IN WITNESS WHEREOF, the undersigned, being the President and the Secretary, respectively, of AMERICAN SOCIETY OF MISSIOLOGY, the unincorporated association which is being incorporated hereby, have executed these Articles of Incorporation.

Bylaws of American Society of Missiology, Inc.

Article I—Principal Office

The principal office for the transaction of the business of the corporation is fixed and located at Pasadena, Los Angeles County, California. The board of directors may at any time or from time to time change the location of the principal office from one location to another in this country.

Article II—Membership

Section 1: Members

There shall be one class of members. Members are those whose dues are paid by the time of the annual meeting of the year to which dues apply.

Section 2: Fees for Membership

The board of directors may recommend to the general membership other classes of members, and the amount, time and manner of payment of initiation and annual dues payable to the corporation by the members. The members at the annual meeting, or at a special meeting called for that purpose shall approve or disapprove the recommendation of the board of directors.

Section 3: Voting Rights of Members

Each member shall be entitled to one vote. Only members may hold office.

Section 4: Liabilities of Members

No person who is now, or who later becomes, a member of this corporation shall be personally liable to its creditors for any indebtedness or liability, and any and all creditors of the corporation shall look only to the assets of this corporation for payment.

Section 5. Sponsors of the American Society of Missiology

An institution or agency may become a sponsor of the American Society of Missiology upon payment of an appropriate amount to be fixed by the board of directors annually. Institutional sponsors shall receive a complimentary subscription to *Missiology: An International Review*.

Article III—Meetings

Section I: Annual Meeting

The annual meeting of the members of the corporation shall be held normally in the month of June in conjunction with the general scholarly meeting of the society.

No notice of any such annual meeting of the members of this corporation need be given if it is held in conjunction with the general scholarly meeting of the society in June of each year: otherwise written notice of the time and place of the annual meeting shall be delivered personally to each voting member or sent to each voting member by mail or other form of written communication, charges prepaid, addressed to him/her at his/her address as it is shown on the records of the corporation, or if it is not shown on the records or is not readily ascertainable, at the place where the meetings of the members are regularly held. Any notice shall be mailed or delivered at least fourteen days before the date of the meeting.

Section 2: Special Meetings

Special meetings of the members of this corporation for any purpose or purposes may be called at any time by the president of the corporation or by any four or more members of the board of directors, or by 10% or more of the members.

Written notice of the time and place of special meetings of the members shall be given in the same manner as for annual meetings of the members.

Section 3: Quorum

A quorum for any meeting of the members shall be a majority of the members present and voting, the minimum being ten members.

Section 4: Adjourned Meetings

Any regular or called meeting of the members may adjourn from day to day, or from time to time, without further notice, until its business is completed.

Section 5: Presiding Officer at Meetings

The president, or, in the absence of the president, the 1st vice president, or the 2nd vice president or in the absence of the president and vice presidents, a chair elected by the members present, shall call the meeting of the members to order, and shall act as the presiding officer thereof. The secretary of the corporation shall act as the secretary of all meetings of the members, and in the absence of the secretary, the presiding officer may appoint any person to act as secretary.

Section 6: Election of the Board of Directors

At the regular annual meeting of the members held normally in the month of June, the members shall elect a board of directors as constituted by these bylaws, and the articles of incorporation of this corporation.

Each year at the annual meeting of the members, the retiring president shall appoint a nominating committee for the coming year and name its chair. Over the course of the year the nominating committee shall develop a slate of candidates for the positions on the board of directors needing to be filled, as well as for the officers, the board of publications, and standing committees of the society. The nominating committee shall make its report at the annual meeting of the members in the following year. At that time, additional nominations may be made from the floor, provided prior agreement has been reached with that nominee that she/he is willing to serve.

Section 7: Proxies

All proxies must be in writing, executed by the members themselves, and must be filed with the secretary of the corporation at or before the meeting of the members.

Article IV—Board of Directors
Section 1: Number of Members of the Board of Directors

The board of directors shall consist of fourteen members until the number is changed by amendment to these bylaws. All members of the board of directors shall be members of this corporation.

Nine of the members are elected as members of the board of directors and the other five, president, two vice presidents, secretary, and treasurer, are on the board of directors by virtue of their offices.

The immediate past president of the American Society of Missiology shall be an advisory member of the board of directors, with voice but not vote.

Section 2: Quorum

A majority of the members of the board of directors shall constitute a quorum for the transaction of business.

Section 3: Powers of the Board of Directors

Subject to the limitations of the articles of incorporation, other sections of the bylaws, and of California law, all corporate powers of the corporation shall be exercised by or under the authority of, and the business affairs of the corporation shall be controlled by the board of directors. Without limiting the general powers, the board of directors shall have the following powers:

1. To select and remove all the other officers, agents, and employees of the corporation, except those specifically elected by the general membership, prescribe such powers and duties for them as may not be inconsistent with law, the articles of incorporation, or the bylaws, fix their compensation, and require from them security for faithful service.
2. To conduct, manage, and control the affairs and business of the corporation, and to make rules and regulations not inconsistent with law, the articles of incorporation or these bylaws.
3. To borrow money and incur indebtedness for the purposes of the corporation, and for that purpose to cause to be executed and delivered, in the corporate name, promissory notes, bonds, debentures, deeds of trust, mortgages, pledges, hypothecations, or other evidence of debt and securities.

Section 4: Decisions of the Board of Directors

All decisions of the board of directors shall be subject to review by the membership.

Section 5: Term of Office

The term of office of each member of the board of directors of this corporation shall be three years or until his/her successor is elected. Successors for members of the board of directors whose terms of office are then expiring shall be elected at the annual meeting of the members in the year in which such terms expire. A member of the board of directors may succeed himself/herself in office.

Section 6: Vacancies

Vacancies in the members of the board of directors shall be filled by a majority of the remaining members then in office. A successor member of the board of directors so elected shall serve for the unexpired term of the predecessor.

Section 7: Place of Meeting

Regular meetings of the board of directors shall be held at any place, within or without the state that has been designated from time to time by resolution of the board of directors or by written consent of all members of the board. In the absence of this designation, regular meetings of the board of directors may be held either at a place designated or at the principal office.

Section 8: Special Meetings

Special meetings of the board of directors may be called at any time for any purpose or purposes by the president or by any three or more members of the board of directors.

Written notice of the time and place of special meetings shall be delivered personally to each member of the board of directors or sent to each member of the board of directors by mail or other form of written communication, charges prepaid, addressed to him/her at his/her address as it is shown on the records of the corporation, or if it is not so shown on the records or is not readily ascertainable, at the place at which the meetings of the board of directors are regularly held. The notice shall be delivered or sent at least fourteen days before the time of the holding of the meeting.

The transactions of any meeting of the board of directors of this corporation, however called and notified, shall be as valid as those at a meeting held after regular call and notice, if a quorum is present, and if, either before or after the meeting, each of the members of the board of directors signs a written waiver of notice, or a consent to holding this meeting, or an approval of the minutes of the meeting. All waivers, consents, or approvals shall be filed with the corporate records or be made a part of the minutes of the meeting.

Section 9: Action without a Meeting

An action by the board of directors may be taken without a meeting if all members of the board of directors individually or collectively consent in writing to this action. Such written consent or consents shall be filed with the minutes of the proceedings of the board of directors.

Section 10: Removal

The board of directors shall have a summary power by vote of a 2/3 majority of its members to suspend, or to expel and terminate the membership of any member of the board of directors for conduct which in its opinion disturbs the order, dignity, business or harmony, or impairs the good name, popularity or prosperity of the organization, or which is likely, in its opinion, to endanger the welfare, interest or character of the organization, or for any conduct in violation of these bylaws or of the rules and regulations of the corporation, which may be made from time to time. Such actions by the board of directors may be taken at any meeting of such committee upon the initiation of any member or members of the committee. The proceedings of the board of directors in such matter shall be final and conclusive.

Section 11: Compensation

The members of the board of directors shall receive no compensation for their services as members of the board of directors except their actual expenses.

Article V—Officers

Section 1: Officers

The officers of this corporation shall be a president, 1st and 2nd vice presidents, secretary, and treasurer, and such other officers as the general membership shall elect, or the board of directors may appoint. The president, vice presidents, secretary, and treasurer shall be members of the board of directors.

Section 2: Election and Terms of Office

At their annual meeting, members of the corporation shall elect the president, 1st vice president, and 2nd vice president. (Nominations for these positions shall reflect the three constituencies from which ASM members come—Roman Catholic, conciliar Protestant, and independent.) The president and two vice presidents shall be elected annually and serve for a term of one year, or until their successors are elected and qualified. It is understood that the vice presidents shall succeed, in turn, to the next office. The secretary and treasurer and all other officers shall serve a term of three years, or until their successors are elected and qualified.

Section 3: Vacancies

A vacancy in any office because of death, resignation, removal, disqualification, or other reason shall be filled by the board of directors.

Section 4: President

Subject to the control of the board of directors, the president shall have general supervision, direction, and control of the business and affairs of the corporation. The president shall preside at all meetings of the members, and of the board of directors, and shall have such other powers and duties as may be prescribed from time to time by the board of directors. The president, with the secretary, shall execute, in the name of the corporation, all deeds, bonds, contracts, and other obligations and instruments authorized by the board of directors to be executed.

The president of the corporation shall be an ex-officio member, with vote, on all committees and boards.

Section 5: Vice President

In the absence or disability of the president, the 1st vice president shall perform all the duties of the president and in so acting shall have all the powers of the president. The 1st vice president shall have such other powers and duties as may be prescribed from time to time by the board of directors.

Section 6: Secretary

The secretary shall keep a full and complete record of the proceedings of the meetings of the members and of the board of directors, shall keep the seal of the corporation and affix it to such papers and instruments as may be required in the regular course of business, shall make service of such notices as may be necessary or proper, shall supervise the keeping of the records of the corporation, shall organize and manage the annual conference and business meeting of the society, shall maintain current membership rolls and bi-annually prepare a membership directory for publication in *Missiology*, shall manage timely communications with the membership, and shall discharge such other duties of the office as prescribed by the board of directors. The secretary may, with the approval of the board of directors, hire the services of an administrative assistant to assist with these duties.

In case of the absence or disability of the secretary, or his/her refusal or neglect to act, notices may be given and served by the president, or by the 1st vice president, or by any person thereunto authorized by the president or by the 1st vice president, or by the board of directors.

Section 7: Treasurer

The treasurer shall receive and safely keep all funds of the corporation and deposit same in such bank or banks as may be designated by the board of directors. These funds shall be paid out only on checks of the corporation signed by the president, 1st vice president, treasurer, or by such officers as may be designated by the board of directors as authorized to sign them.

The treasurer shall also keep careful financial records of the society's income and expenditure, and arrange for an annual financial report to be professionally prepared; present the annual financial report to the board of directors and make it available to the ASM membership to review; prepare for the board of directors and the society a proposed budget for the ensuing year; issue tax-related documents in a timely manner; arrange for the timely preparation and submission of appropriate state and federal tax forms; promptly reimburse persons for any legitimate society expenses; maintain the financial files of the society, including tax returns, receipts of expenditures, 1099 forms, and any correspondence with the IRS; coordinate the processes for receiving *Missiology* subscriptions and membership dues. The treasurer may, with the approval of the board of directors, hire the services of an administrative assistant to assist with these duties.

Article VI—Board of Publications and Standing Committees

Section I: Board of Publications

The board of publications shall consist of twelve (12) members, including nine (9) members who shall serve terms of three years and three ex-officio members: the president, the secretary and the treasurer. A member of the board of publications may succeed himself/herself in office.

Section 2: Publisher

The publisher shall be elected by the board of publications for a 3-year term. The person may be re-elected.

Section 3: Editorial Policies

Policies concerning the publications shall be determined by the board of publications, subject to review by the membership at the annual meeting.

Section 4. Management of ASM Publications

The board of publications appoints persons to manage each of the ASM's publication areas as editors and editorial committees. These areas of publication, with brief descriptions of their aims, are as follows:

Missiology: An International Review is a peer-reviewed scholarly quarterly journal that publishes articles on the full range of practical and theoretical issues that are the subject matter of the discipline of missiology and mission studies. The editor of *Missiology* reports to the board of publications through the publisher.

The ASM Series publishes books of a scholarly nature in association with a publisher whose list is respected in the academic world in an effort to bring works of mission studies into the wider theological conversation. The ASM Series Editorial Committee reports to the board of publications through the publisher.

The ASM Scholarly Monograph Series publishes dissertations and other works of a specialized nature in mission studies to make such work available to its appropriate readership. The ASM Scholarly Monograph Series reports to the board of publications through the publisher.

The ASM Electronic Media Committee has responsibility (1) for the design and upkeep of the society's website as a resource for the society itself and to provide information on the society for all who seek it; (2) for the electronic publication of materials such as, but not limited to, issues of *Missiology*, the society's other publications; and (3) for electronic forums on matters of interest to the society and mission studies. The ASM Electronic Media Committee reports directly to the board of publications.

In the event of a vacancy in the positions of editors or editorial committees, a nominating committee of the board of publications shall be appointed by the chair of the board of publications that shall consist of the American Society of Missiology publisher and one person each from the three society constituencies (Roman Catholic, conciliar Protestant, and independent) who are members of the board of publications. The chair of the board of publications will be an ex officio member of the nominating committee. Other members may be appointed to the nominating committee in order to provide balance in constituency representation. The nominating committee will submit its nomination to the board of publications for its action.

Section 5: Election

Members of the board of publications are elected by members of the society present at its annual meeting. The nominating committee appointed by the president (as described in Article III, Section 6) shall propose a slate of candidates for the positions on the board of publications to be filled. Additional nominations may be made from the floor when the nominating committee makes its report, provided prior agreement has been reached with that nominee that he/she is willing to so serve.

Section 6: Organization of the Board of Publications

The board of publications shall organize itself by election of its own officers.

Section 7: Standing Committees of the Society

Standing committees of the society may be established as deemed necessary by the board of directors or by the membership at the annual meeting. Once established, standing committees shall organize themselves by election of their own officers.

Article VII—Seal

The board of directors shall provide a suitable seal for the corporation.

Article VIII—Amendment of Bylaws

These bylaws may be amended or repealed and new bylaws adopted by the vote of the majority of the members of the board of directors at any board of directors meeting, excepted that a bylaw fixing or changing the number of the members of the board of directors may be adopted, amended or repealed only by the vote or written consent of a majority of the members of the corporation called for that purpose and which is a majority of the vote of those present and voting. Any amendment to these bylaws adopted by the board of directors shall be binding on the members unless and until rejected by the voting members at an annual meeting of the members or a special meeting of the members called for that purpose. It shall be the duty of the board of directors to present to the members for ratification or rejection at each annual meeting of the members, or at any special meeting held in lieu of an annual meeting, amendments to the bylaws that have been made by the board of directors during the year immediately preceding the annual meeting.

Article IX—Records and Inspections

Section 1: Records

The corporation shall maintain adequate and correct accounts, books and records of its business and properties. All of such books, records and accounts shall be kept at its principal place of business in the state of California, or as fixed by the board of directors from time to time.

Section 2: Inspection of Books and Records

All books and records of the corporation shall be open to inspection by the members of the board of directors at all reasonable times at the principal office of the corporation.

Section 3: Inspection and Certification of Bylaws

The original or a copy of these bylaws as amended or otherwise altered to date, certified by the secretary, shall be open to inspection by the members of the corporation as provided in Section 502 of the corporations code of California.

Section 4: Annual Reports

The board of directors shall cause an annual report to be made to the members not later than the annual meeting following the close of the fiscal year. Said annual report shall contain a balance sheet as of the closing date of such year, together with a statement of income and profit and loss for such year. These financial statements shall be certified by the president, the treasurer, or a public accountant.

Article X—Fiscal Year

The fiscal year of this corporation shall be January 1 to December 31. Certified as amended June 16, 2012.

Appendix F

Key dates in the history
of the American Society of Missiology

1917   The Fellowship of Professors of Missions of the Atlantic Seaboard was founded.

1921   The Lux Mundi (LM) group was founded.

1952   The Association of Professors of Missions (APM) was founded.

1965   The Association of Evangelical Professors of Missions (AEPM) was founded.

1972   A meeting was convened to prepare for founding of American Society of Missiology.

1972   The International Association of Mission Studies (IAMS) was founded.

1972   The bimonthly *Practical Anthropology* ceased publication after nineteen years.

1973   The ASM journal *Missiology: An International Review* began publication.

1973   The ASM organizing meeting was held in June.

1974   Constitution and bylaws of the ASM were adopted.

1976   The ASM became a constituent member of the Council on the Study of Religion (CSR), later renamed Council of Societies for the Study of Religion.

1980   First two volumes in American Society of Missiology monograph series were published.

1997   First two volumes were published in ASM dissertation series.

2004	ASM ended membership in Council of Societies for the Study of Religion (CSSR).
2011	Gerald H. Anderson was given Lifetime Achievement Award.
2012	James A. Scherer was given Lifetime Achievement Award.
2012	Final annual meeting held at Techny Towers, Techny, IL, marked twenty-five years since the founding of the ASM.

References cited

American Society of Missiology (ASM) records
 1973– The Billy Graham Center Archives in Wheaton, Illinois, is the permanent repository for official ASM records.
Anderson, Gerald H.
 1973 "Introducing Missiology." *Missiology* 1, no. 1 (January): 3–5.
 1987 Background to the Founding of the American Society of Missiology. Personal recollections recorded on tape January 10, 1987; in author's possession.
 2012 *Witness to World Christianity: The International Association for Mission Studies, 1972–2012.* New Haven, CT: OMSC Publications.
Anderson, Gerald H., ed.
 1998 *Biographical Dictionary of Christian Missions.* New York: Macmillan Reference USA.
Barrett, David B.
 1987 "Forecasting the Future in World Mission." *Missiology* 15, no. 4 (October): 433–50.
Barrett, David B., ed.
 1982 *World Christian Encyclopedia: A Comparative Study of Churches and Religions in the Modern World, AD 1900–2000.* Nairobi: Oxford University Press.
Barrett, David B., George Thomas Kurian, and Todd M. Johnson, eds.
 2001 *World Christian Encyclopedia: A Comparative Survey of Churches and Religions in the Modern World.* 2nd ed. 2 vols. Oxford: Oxford University Press.

Beaver, R. Pierce
  1968   "The Meaning and Place of Missiology Today in the American Scene." Manuscript in American Society of Missiology records.
  1976   "The American Protestant Theological Seminary and Missions: An Historical Survey." *Missiology* 4, no. 1 (January 1976): 75–87.
  1979   "The Purpose and History of the American Society of Missiology." Manuscript in American Society of Missiology records.
Beaver, R. Pierce, ed.
  1977   *American Missions in Bicentennial Perspective.* South Pasadena: William Carey Library.
Bevans, Stephen B., and Roger P. Schroeder
  2004   *Constants in Context: A Theology of Mission for Today.* Maryknoll, NY: Orbis Books.
Bosch, David J.
  1991   *Transforming Mission: Paradigm Shifts in Theology of Mission.* Maryknoll, NY: Orbis Books.
Bühlmann, Walbert
  1976   *The Coming of the Third Church: An Analysis of the Present and Future of the Church.* Slough: St. Paul Publications.
Catholic Church
  1976   *On Evangelization in the Modern World: Apostolic Exhortation Evangelii nuntiandi*, December 8, 1975. Washington: Publications Office, United States Catholic Conference.
  1990   *Encyclical letter Redemptoris missio of the Supreme Pontiff John Paul II on the Permanent Validity of the Church's Missionary Mandate.* Washington, DC: United States Catholic Conference.
Coe, Shoki
  1972   "Contextualizing Theology." *Mission Trends* 3, edited by Gerald H. Anderson and Thomas Stransky, 19–24. Grand Rapids, MI: Wm. B. Eermans, 1976.
Corrie, John, ed.
  2007   *Dictionary of Mission Theology: Evangelical Foundations.* Nottingham, England: InterVarsity Press.

Damboriena, Prudencio, SJ

1971   "Aspects of the Missionary Crisis in Roman Catholicism." In *The Future of the Christian World Mission*, edited by William J. Danker and Wi Jo Kang, 73–87. Grand Rapids, MI: Wm. B. Eerdmans.

Dries, Angelyn, OSF

1998   *The Missionary Movement in American Catholic History, 1820–1980.* Maryknoll, NY: Orbis Books.

Dyrness, William A., and Veli-Matti Kärkkäinen, eds.

2008   *Global Dictionary of Theology: A Resource for the Worldwide Church.* Downers Grove, IL: IVP Academic.

Fairbank, John King

1969   "Assignment for the '70s." *American Historical Review* 74, no. 3 (February): 861–79.

Flett, John G.

2010   *The Witness of God: The Trinity, Missio Dei, Karl Barth, and the Nature of Christian Community.* Grand Rapids, MI: Wm. B. Eerdmans.

Glasser, Arthur F.

1980   "Archival Alert—Rome 1980." *Missiology* 8, no. 4 (October): 389–95.

Guder, Darrell L., ed.

1998   *Missional Church: A Vision for the Sending of the Church in North America.* Grand Rapids, MI: Wm. B. Eerdmans.

Gutiérrez, Gustavo

1973   *A Theology of Liberation: History, Politics, and Salvation.* Maryknoll, NY: Orbis Books.

Hanciles, Jehu J.

2008   *Beyond Christendom: Globalization, African Migration, and the Transformation of the West.* Maryknoll, NY: Orbis Books.

Hassing, Per, and Donald M. Wodarz, SSC

1972   Letter (March 9) on behalf of Boston Theological Institute. In American Society of Missiology records.

Hesselgrave, David J.

1983   "The AEPM: An Evangelical Alternative." *Trinity World Forum* 9, no. 1.

1984 "AEPM News and Views." *Evangelical Missions Quarterly* 20, no. 1 (January).

Horner, Norman A.

1987 "The Association of Professors of Missions: The First Thirty-Five Years, 1952–1987." *International Bulletin of Missionary Research* 11, no. 3 (July): 120–24.

International Congress on World Evangelization

1990 *Proclaim Christ until He Comes: Calling the Whole Church to Take the Whole Gospel to the Whole World.* The Second Lausanne Congress. Minneapolis, MN: World Wide Publications.

2010 *The Cape Town Commitment: A Confession of Faith and a Call to Action.* The Third Lausanne Congress. Online: http://www.lausanne.org/en/documents/ctcommitment.html.

Irvin, Dale T., and Scott W. Sunquist

2001 *History of the World Christian Movement.* Vol. 1: *Earliest Christianity to 1453.* Maryknoll, NY: Orbis Books.

2012 *History of the World Christian Movement.* Vol. 2: *Modern Christianity from 1454 to 1800.* Maryknoll, NY: Orbis Books.

Irvine, Cecilia

1976 "Documentation of Mission in the Nineteenth and Twentieth Centuries." *Missiology* 4, no. 2 (April): 189–205.

Jackson, Herbert C.

1967 "The Association of Professors of Missions." In *The Encyclopedia of Modern Christian Missions,* edited by Burton Goddard. Camden, NJ: Thomas Nelson & Sons.

Kraft, Charles H.

1979 *Christianity in Culture: A Study in Dynamic Biblical Theologizing in Cross-Cultural Perspective.* Maryknoll, NY: Orbis Books.

2005 *SWM/SIS at Forty: A Participant/Observer's View of Our History.* Pasadena: William Carey Library.

Lacy, Creighton

1970 "The Association of Professors of Missions." In *Concise Dictionary of the Christian World Mission,* edited by Stephen

Neill, Gerald H. Anderson, and John Godwin. London: USCL/Lutterworth Press; Nashville: Abingdon Press.

Latourette, Kenneth Scott

1967   *Beyond the Ranges.* Grand Rapids, MI: Wm. B. Eerdmans.

Luzbetak, Louis J.

1976   "Missiology Comes of Age." *Missiology* 4, no. 1 (January): 11–12.

1988   *The Church and Cultures: New Perspectives in Missiological Anthropology.* Maryknoll, NY: Orbis Books.

Moffett, Samuel Hugh

1987   "Early Asian Christian Approaches to Non-Christian Cultures." *Missiology* 15, no. 4 (October): 473–86.

Montgomery, Robert L.

1986   "Receptivity to an Outside Religion: Light from Interaction between Sociology and Missiology." *Missiology* 14, no. 3 (July): 287–99.

1999   *Introduction to the Sociology of Missions.* Westport, CT: Praeger.

Moreau, A. Scott, Harold A. Netland, Charles Edward van Engen, and David Burnett, eds.

2000   *Evangelical Dictionary of World Missions.* Grand Rapids, MI: Baker Books.

Müller, Karl, Theo Sundermeier, Stephen B. Bevans, and Richard Bliese, eds.

1999   *Dictionary of Mission: Theology, History, Perspectives.* Maryknoll, NY: Orbis Books.

Myklebust, Olav Guttorm

1955,   *The Study of Missions in Theological Education.* 2 vols. Oslo:
1957   Forlaget Land of Kirke Egede Institute.

1986   "On the Origin of IAMS." *Mission Studies* 3, no. 4–11.

Newbigin, Lesslie

1983   *The Other Side of 1984: Questions for the Churches.* Geneva: World Council of Churches.

Robert, Dana L.

1996   *American Women in Mission: A Social History of Their Thought and Practice.* Macon, GA: Mercer University Press.

2003   *Occupy until I Come: A. T. Pierson and the Evangelization of the World.* Library of Religious Biography. Grand Rapids, MI: Wm. B. Eerdmans.

Roxburgh, John
2012   "Rescuing the Memory of Mission." In *Witness to World Christianity: The International Association for Mission Studies, 1972–2012,* edited by Gerald H. Anderson, 133–56. New Haven, CT: OMSC Publications.

Sanneh, Lamin
1989   *Translating the Message: The Missionary Impact on Culture.* Maryknoll, NY: Orbis Books.

Scherer, James A.
1971   "Missions in Theological Education." In *The Future of the Christian World Mission,* edited by William J. Danker and Wi Jo Kang, 143–53. Grand Rapids, MI: Wm. B. Eerdmans.

Schreiter, Robert J.
1985   *Constructing Local Theologies.* Maryknoll, NY: Orbis Books.

Shenk, Wilbert R.
1985   "The Contribution of Henry Venn to Mission Thought." *Anvil* 2, no. 1:25–42.
2010   "Dr. Ralph D. Winter and the American Society of Missiology." *Missiology* 38, no. 1 (January): 92–93.

Speer, Robert E.
1902   "The Science of Missions." In *Missionary Principles and Practice,* 43–68. New York: Fleming H. Revell.

Stowe, David M.
1967   "Changing Patterns of Missionary Service in Today's World." *Occasional Bulletin of Missionary Research* 20, no. 1 (January): 1–10.

Stransky, Thomas F.
1982   "Evangelization, Missions, and Social Action: A Roman Catholic Perspective." *Review and Expositor* 79, no. 2 (April): 343–50.

Thomas, Norman E.
1986   "Selected Annotated Bibliography of Missiology." *Missiology* 14, no. 1 (January): 91–92.

1987   "The ASM Bibliography Project on Missiology." *Mission Studies* IV-2 (8): 74.

1988   "Projected Media in Mission Archives and Documentation." *Mission Studies* V-2 (10): 136–41.

Verkuyl, J.

1978   *Contemporary Missology: An Introduction*. Grand Rapids, MI: Wm. B. Eerdmans.

Walls, Andrew F.

1996   *The Missionary Movement in Christian History: Studies in the Transmission of Faith*. Maryknoll, NY: Orbis Books.

Winter, Ralph D.

1972   "Mini-Publishing: New Hope for Strategic Dialogue." *Occasional Bulletin from the Missionary Research Library* 23, no. 2 (February).

1984   "There's a place for the AEPM." *Evangelical Missions Quarterly* 20, no. 3 (July): 274–75.

1987   Personal communication. May 7.

Woodberry, J. Dudley, Charles Edward van Engen, and Edgar J. Elliston, eds.

1996   *Missiological Education for the Twenty-First Century: The Book, the Circle, and the Sandals: Essays in Honor of Paul E. Pierson*. Maryknoll, NY: Orbis Books.

World Council of Churches

1982   "Mission and Evangelism: An Ecumenical Affirmation." Online: http://www.religion-online.org/showchapter.asp?title=1573&C=1525.

World Missionary Conference (WMC)

1910   *The Homebase*. Report of Commission VI. Edinburgh/London: Oliphant, Ferrier and Anderson.

Wright, Christopher J. H.

2006   *The Mission of God: Unlocking the Bible's Grand Narrative*. Downers Grove, IL: IVP Academic.